PATRIOTISM

PATRIOTISM

PATRICIA BAMURANGIRWA

Matador
9 Priory Business Park
Kibworth Beauchamp
Leicestershire LE8 0RX, UK
Tel: (+44) 116 279 2299
Fax: (+44) 116 279 2277
Email: books@troubador.co.uk
Web: www.troubador.co.uk/matador

ISBN 978-1784621-421

British Library Cataloguing in Publication Data.
A catalogue record for this book is available from the British Library.

Printed and bound in the UK by TJ International, Padstow, Cornwall
Typeset in 11pt Bembo by Troubador Publishing Ltd, Leicester, UK

Matador is an imprint of Troubador Publishing Ltd

CONTENTS

RWANDA

Rwanda rwange Rwanda nkunda
Rwanda rwambyaye uzamporana
Igihe cyose nzaba nkiliho Rwanda
Reka nkuzirikane warampetse
Nzakuraga abankomokaho bose Rwanda rwiza
Aho bazaba bali hose bajje bakulilimba
Bajje bamenya ko bakomoka murwagasabo

Rwanda rwange uteye ubwuzu
Ufite ubwiza bwifuzwa nabenchi
Butarubwi Ingagi gusa Rwanda.
Ufite isuku hose mulibyose.
Dore ko wiyemeje guca ruswa
ahubwo ukarangwa niyosuku muribyose

Abakugenda barabirata
Bati Urwanda rwubu nurundi
Rukoresha ubumenyi sicyimenyane
Benerwo alibo babiteye
Bazi ko gukora arugukorana umwete
Ugakora wikorera akimuhana kakibagirana

Ntibakina ngo bakinishe igihe
Kuko bazi ko iyo cyigiye cyitagaruka

1

Bagikoresha neza nubushishozi
Bo bati twe turubaka twiyubakira
Bizigaragaze uzashobora aduhe umuganda
Nubusangwe ngo ntawurata inkongoro yumwana
Kuko uyinweramo aba ayigaragaza.

Bati reka tuzasige amateka
Azaba ateye ishema nubwuzu
Abazaza ejo bazasange twarabateganirije.
Bazaturate baturirimbe
bati abakurambere bacu bari bamudatenguha.

Baje alingenzi nibo dukesha ibi byose
Baharaniye kudusigira umuganda
Bakadusigira Urwanda rwindatwa.
Bakadusigira urwambaye ikamba
Baharanire gushinga ikirenge mucyanyu.
Yenda bo bati reka tunabarenze kubera ibihe tugezemo.

Abanyura mukirere cyarwo bajja ahandi
Barebera kure uko rushashagirana
Bakibagirwa ko bali mukirere cya Afrika
Babwirwa ko ali Kigali banyuze hejuru bakumirwa
Bikazabatera kuzaza bazanwe nokuhitegereza

Bahagera bagasanga batarabeshwe
Bati ibyo batubwiye turabibonye
Ko Urwanda ruteye ubwizu mulibyose.
Abakobwa beza bakwakirana icyinyabuphura

Aho bakwacyirira heza huzuye ituze
Harangwa nisuku ikwiranye nabo.
Imisozi yaho ifutse yizihiye amaso.

Uti sinzataha ntayigaraguyemo
Ubwo ukayiterera bigatinda
Ukajja nogusura izo Ngagi zarwo ziswe amazina.
Kandi ubwo ulinzwe bitagukanga.

Abakulinze muvugana buvandimwe
Alingabo zihagatiye imiheto.
Muvugana bucuti ugasanga byose byakurenze.
Igihe cyawe cyogutaha uti nsige ibi nsange ibihe
Ukababara ntibibe ibanga
Ubwo ntibube ubwamyuma kuhagenda
Ukajja agaruka cyanga ukanahatura
Hakaba nubwo akenchi uhashaka umugeni
Kubera ubwo bwiza bwabanyampinga.

Umva Rwanda ubu wabaye icyamamare
Kandi numurage birasanzwe
Ko utajja uheranwa namakuba
Ibyo arikizira
Uhindura isura mwidakika
Ugahindura ishusho ihesha abawe ishema
Hakaba hamamazwa ubutwari niterambere.
Amacakubiri yamaze abantu
Muti ibyabyo
Mubirebe munyandiko

Abashyitsi basanga inseko yabarutuye.

Basanga ubyina udasobanya Rwanda
Ryacurabulindi ryitsemba bantu ryabaye inkuru
Bati Urwanda rwateye ikirenge mucya Kirenga
Uratera intambwe wungikanya
Urasa nuvuruganya inka ikamwa neza
Ahubwo iryavuzwe ryaratashye
Wabaye ishuli ryamahanga
Ayakure nayahafi

Baraza kukwigiraho iterambere nituze
Ndetse kubera impuhwe ukanajjayo kuberekera
Ukaberekera ukanabarinda amakuba
Dore ko ribara uwariraye
Uti nchuti zacu tuzabigishya
Kandi tunabarinde mugire amahoro nkatwe

Impamo ikigaragaza rugikubita
Rwanda iti nimworoshye mwitangara
Iri nisiza ridasubira inyuma.
Bwabutwari bwumurage bukabajja imbere
Hose aho mutungutse bati uru nirwo Rwanda

Ngaho Sudani, Liberia
Ndetse nomubirwa bya Haiti
Nahandi henchi cyane
Muti tuzabaha urugero rwubugenge
Kuko mufite inyota yokumenya ibyacu.

Tuzaza tubegere tubavungurireho
Tubigishe ibyigishwa
Ibindi tubitahane kuko nikamere
 bitubamo ibyo ntitubitanga
Numurage twarazwe
nabakurambere bacu.

Reka nguhurizeho inganzo Rwanda
ngutake kuko ubikwiye
Warahiye ko utazamera nkamahanga
Abahora murufaya rwokwihugiraho baramya ifaranga
Inshuti zabo zikaba imbwa na terevizio
Aribyo ifaranga ryabatoranirije rimaze kubaca kubandi.
Yenda nibyo barazwe nababo.

Aliko Rwanda uti sinzahara imico yange

Yubutwari buririmbwa hose
Bubagarwa nubumwe nurukundo
Nzaguhunda amasaro namasimbi Rwanda rwange
Nzakwambika IKAMBA rigukwiye ube urwema mumahanga
Nzagukenyeza ubumwe ngutere urukundo Rwanda

Interuro yawe itangaza amahanga
Watangiye kwitwa Kirenga
Mumyaka izaza uzaba ikirangirire kwisi hose
Kandi nubundi byarabaye
Nko kumenya akamaro kabari nabategarugore.
Ubu umukobwa aravugwa rikumvwa
Aliko igihe avuga ukuli niterambere

Avuga irikwiye, ntirifefekwa ngo kuko
arumukobwa.
Iteka werekana ko ubizi
ko
ngo ukurusha urugo nuko aba akurusha umugore
Kubazinzizika warabyanze
Uzi ko bakunda ababo kuko ali nabo babaheka.
Ubagereranya na Nyirabiyoro na Ndabaga

Mvuze imihigo yanyu bwakwira bugacya
Ese ninde utasamazwa nokukureba
Rwanda

Ngo avugishwe nubwo bwiza nimyifatire?

Abawe aho turi Ibulayi cyanga ahandi
tuba tugukumbuye Rurangaza
Kubera urukundo duhorana rwadushegeshe
Uje kugusura arisukura akaza wese
Akararama akarangara, ntarambirwe kukureba

Yaba azanye nabatakuzi agahuzwa nokukurata
Kandi Rwanda nawe uba umukumbuye cyane.
Dore ko umuhobera abo arikumwe nabo
nabarebera hirya bikabarangaza, ibineza bikabasaba.
Rwanda ukamwakira nkuwawe, bati ese uyu ninde uje aho
akunzwe

Ati mwitangara naje iwacu
Mpakumbuye naho aruko

Ati nikoko naje aho nkunzwe
Ubwo agatangira kubwira Urwanda
ko ntahindutse ntahungabanye.
Ngo yenda naba naranyeganyejwe namahanga.
Akandemura uko Gihanga yampanze.

Ati humura Rwanda ukunze ugukunze
Ntugahinde umushyitsi umfite
Ntugahindurwe ntukigunge duhali
Uradufite tuzagusokoza ibisage
Dore abawe barakwambika urugukwiye
Indoro ningendo uteye imbabazi

Imihigo yabawe nukuzakuragira
dore ko banabinwereye igihango Rwanda
Ko bazakulinda ibisambo nibisahiranda
Bazakumara irungu useke ucye kumutima
Kandi ntanuwo bazatuma aba igihangange
mumahanga yaraguhemukiye Rwanda.

Babandi batishimira ko ugira abahanga,
ngo ugire IBANGA,
ugire abahanzi ugire IBAMBE
kandi arumurage wurwa Gasabo.
Bazatsindwe na GIHANGA.
Urwanda rukomeze imitsindo
ababyeyi bari kukiriri baruhuke
Bishimire kungura imiryango
Bonse abakura bazitwa ba Kavuna
Abangavu bakomeze bambare amasimbi batete

Intwari zawe zasibuye imiringoti
Yari yamariwemo abawe
Zateyemo indabyo hose
Dore urushashagirana urinyabagendwa.

Zarababariye bitavanze nokwibagirwa
Ngo hatazagira ikizongera kuguhungabanya Rwanda
Hatazagira uwakongera gutinyuka gutokoza ubwo buranga
Naragukunze ndaranguza Rwanda
Byanteye nogukunda wese uzagukunda

Dore ngo Rurema Aragaragariza ISI yose
Ko Urwanda arintore yahisemo.
Rurema ati nubwo Urwanda ndugize igihugu gito mubugari
Ariko ndugize agasongero KISI
Rube ikirunga kiruka amahoro
Azajja anyanyagira mubange
Mpisemo kurugira isoko yubuzima

Isoko izatunga abantu ninyamaswa

Iyo soko izava mu Rwanda kugera kure cyane
Kugirango izahe ubuzima abiyo
Ayo mazi y'Urwanda yiswe Nile
Agera Ethiopia
Nomuli Misili ayo mazi yacu atanga imigisha
Yuhagira abageni nabavutse.
Akuhagira ababyeyi agahembura abarwaye
Dore ko yanuhagiye umwana wabaye ikirangilire
Nanubu akivugwa hose

Ubwo umwana Yezu Crhist ababyeyi be
bashakira amahoro mu Misiri
Yuhagiwe na Nile ituruka
mwishyamba ryinzitane rya Nyungwe.
Ababyeyi babaririje ayo mazi meza azira
umuze aho akomoka
Bati ava kure cyane Yezu azahamenya akuze
Bati nahahanzwe na Gihanga hahawe imigisha
Bati inkomoko yayo mazi ibarizwa i Rwanda

Ntanahandi yakabaye ,ntahandi yalikwiye
Ibyo mwarabyiboneye kuko Rurema Atavuguruzwa
Ubwo yavugze ati: Urwanda nirubumbatira iyosoko

Dore ko nijjeze kurota inzozi zikaba impamo
Narose abangavu nabari bateye imbabazi
Ndota intore zarangaje abazireba
Ndota Urucanda nurucanzogera,
ndota abakambwe nababyeyi bambaye ingore bizihiwe

Ndota batanga impundu murwa Gasabo kandi baseka bose
bashimishijwe nuko batuje bari mubitaramo baririrmba
bagutaka Rwanda

Bati tugize amahirwe yokurubona urwahanuwe ruzaba
rutemba amata nubuki
nuru.
Genda Rwanda ufite igikundiro kigukwiye.

RWANDA

My Rwanda, Rwanda I love.
Rwanda who bore me, you will carry me always.
All the time I shall live Rwanda
Let me cling on you, you carried me on your back
I shall give you inheritance of all my descendants
Beautiful Rwanda.
My Rwanda you are full of joy
You are full of beauty which is desired by many
Not only for gorillas Rwanda
You are clean in everything
You have sworn to fight corruption
You are known for your cleanliness in all.
Your visitors praise it
That Rwanda of today is different
It uses knowledge not favouritism
Its citizens are the cause of this
They know that working needs to be interesting
You work with zeal for yourself and forget to wait from
    anywhere else
They don't play with time
They know that time wasted never comes back
They use it usefully with intelligence

They say that we build for ourselves
Let it be shown and those interested will assist us.
Originally no one praises a baby's milk bottle
Because the baby using it displays it all.
Let us set law and order
They will be full of joy and zeal
The next generation will find order
They will congratulate and praise us
That our elders were not disobedient
They came as genius and we owe them all this.
They struggled to leave us collective work
They left us a Rwanda worth being proud of
They shall yearn to follow in your footsteps
Perhaps they shall struggle to go a step forward because of
    the current development
Those travelling by air going elsewhere
They view its shining beauty from afar
They forget that they are in an African airspace
When they are told that it's the view of Kigali they wonder
This forces them to purposely visit the place and have a close
    view of it.
When they reach Kigali they are satisfied and believe what
    they saw
That we have physically seen what we are told, that Rwanda
    is full of joy and zeal in all
Beautiful girls welcome you with respect
The place where they welcome you is full of comfort
It is displayed with the cleanliness befitting them
Its covered hills please the eyes
I swear not to return home before I rest in these hills

You visit them and spend good time
You also visit gorillas which have been named
Remember you are guarded in a friendly way
The guards carrying their arrows
You are conversing with the guards like brothers and sisters
    and you feel overwhelmed
When time comes to return home you feel like not leaving
    all these beauties
You feel sad without hiding it
And this will not be the last time to visit
You keep on coming back to visit or you even settle
    permanently
In most cases you decide to marry from this place
Because of the beauty of those Rwandan daughters
Here Rwanda you've become now praise (Model)
And this is inherited and is normal
That you have never got washed away with troubles
That has never happened
Rwanda you change your appearance in just a minute
You change an image that gives pride to your people
Your might and development shall be praised
Divisions have made people perish
That their business
Read them in history
Visitors find laughter amongst the citizens
They find you dancing without tarnishing Rwanda
Genocide became news worldwide
Rwanda has stepped a milestone to change to its best
You make a step one by one
You look like a milking cow that gives milk in full capacity

In fact what was predicted has come to pass
You've become a lesson to other countries
Distant and nearby countries
They come to learn developmental programmes and peace
    from you
And because of your goodness and pity you visit them and
    demonstrate to them.
You demonstrate and guard them from troubles
You know experience is the best teacher
Come on our friends we shall teach you
And we shall guard you so that you have peace like us.
The truth is shown after troubles start
Rwanda said you wait do not worry or wonder
This is a movement which does not move backward
The inherited bravery leads them
Wherever you reach they admit that this is the real Rwanda
There is Liberia and Sudan, even in Haiti Islands among
    other countries my Rwanda.
You said that you shall give them an example of
    independence
Since you are thirsty of knowing our programmes
We shall come near you and give you some
We shall teach you what is necessary
We shall return with some which is culture
This lives in us, we do not give it away
This is an inheritance given to us by our ancestors
Let me gather my conquest on you Rwanda
Let me decorate you because you are worthy of it.
You swore not to be like other countries
Those who live in conflicts

Adoring money
When best friends are dogs and televisions
That is what money chose for them, separating them from
    others.
Maybe it is their inheritance from their ancestors
But as for me Rwanda I will not drop my culture
Of bravery and heroism which is praised everywhere
Weeded by unity and love
I will decorate you with beads.
I will decorate you with a crown that you deserve so that you
    become outstanding to other countries
I will dress you with unity and lead you with love Rwanda
You're beginning to impress other countries
You've started being called Supreme
In the coming years you will be a Super Power in the whole
    world.
In fact it has already happened
Like identifying the rights of men and women
Now ladies have freedom of speech
But only when she speaks the truth and development
When she speaks the fact, and it's not ignored because she is
    a woman
You always display your knowledge
That the one who has the best home has the best wife.
You refused to keep hatred
You know that they love their own because they nurtured
    them.

You equate them to Nyirabiyoro and Ndabaga
If I started narrating your praises it would take day and night

Who shall not wonder to see you Rwanda?
To talk about your beauty and behaviour
Yours who are in Europe or other countries
We miss you extremely
Because of lots of love that we have for you
Whoever comes to visit you cleans and comes whole
heartedly
He stares and wonders without getting tired of looking at you
If he/she comes with first time visitors, he/she is overtaken
by praise
And you Rwanda miss us too much
You hug them and all the visitors and those watching from a
distance
Are surprised and they are full of happiness
Rwanda you welcome them like your own
And ask who is this one who has come where they are loved?
Don't be surprised they have come home, they miss it
It is true they have come to where they are loved
I immediately begin my conversation with Rwanda
That I did not change or become shaken
That maybe I might have been overtaken by the foreign
countries
And change me from the way the creator had created me
Be calm Rwanda you love whoever loves you
Do not tremble when you have me
Do not fumble and get sad when we are here
You have us around. We shall comb your hair
Look, your own dresses you smartly
Your looks and movements lead to mercy
The promises of your own are to shepherd you

Even a pact was made for that, Rwanda,
That they will guard you from thieves and selfish people
They will end your loneliness
You will laugh and get a clean heart
And nobody will be allowed to be above others
He disappointed you in foreign countries
Those who are not happy for you to have genius
So that you can have a secret
To have manufacturers and have peace
Let them be defeated by the creator
Rwanda continue with visitors
Mothers who are in labour have rest
Let them be happy of multiplying families
Let them breastfed the growing
And they will be called the unbreakable.
Let young girls continue wearing gems and get spoiled
Your heroes dug out or excavated the lost
It had been drowned by your people
Flowers were planted in them
They forgave without forgetting
So that there will not be anything that will shake you again
So that nobody will dare to spoil its beauty
Rwanda I over-loved you
It led me to love whoever will love you
Look how the creator lightens the whole world
That Rwanda is chosen among others
The creator said that though I have made Rwanda a small
    country in length
But I am making it the top of the world
Let it be a chain that chains peace

That will be spreading among my people
I choose to make it the source of life
The source which will keep people and animals
The source will come from Rwanda and will reach very far
So that it can give life to the people there
That Rwanda water will be called the Nile
It will reach Ethiopia
Up to Egypt that water of ours gives blessings
It baths the brides and the newborn
It births the mothers and heals the sick
It even bathed the child who was proclaimed
Even now he is still being proclaimed everywhere
When Jesus Christ's parents looking for peace in Egypt
Were bathed with Nile coming from Nyungwe forest
His parents enquired where this clean water
Without blemishes was coming from
And they said that it comes from very far
Jesus will know the place when he grows up.
That the place was created by the Creator and was given
    blessings
That the source of that water is aquired from Rwanda
Nowhere else it could be and nowhere else is it supposed to
    be.
The Creator said let Rwanda hold the source of life
Look I am sure the dreams I had were true
I dreamed about the clean and the merciful
I dreamed about dancers
Who puzzled those who were looking at them
I dreamed about the toddlers and leg bells
I dreamed about elders and parents

Wearing beautiful crowns
I dreamed seeing them shouting praises in
Rwagasabo's place and all of them were laughing
They were happy because they were telling stories
Singing and praising Rwanda
Which we are lucky to see the Rwanda
That was prophesied
To be a country where milk and honey will be flowing.
Go Rwanda you are worthy to be loved.

KAGAME

Ndumuhanzi uhanga ibiriho
Reka mbabwire Paul Kagame uko namubonye
Ibyo muvuga sibishyitsi
Murasanga aliko mumuzi
Agira igihagararo kikirenga
Akagira ijisho rikanga ababisha.

Nirugamburuza bagambanyi
Ni Kagame kananiye abagome
Iyanezerewe aramwenyura
Kandi agira ninseko nziza.

Ariko yanga udufuti akanga amafuti
ndetse akanga nabayakunda
arabanza akabigisha
akabiyegereza.
Ati ndumuzira futi niko navutse
Dore ko ntawabimuhora ariko yahanzwe.

Rurema yamugize intore
amugira Rutinwa
Amwambika igitinyiro
gikwiye Urwanda.

Amugira ikirezi cyu Urwagasabo
nabarukunda.

Dore ko yanga abavuga urukonjo
nikonjokonjo.
Ibiri mumatamatama bitumvwa
Ngo bibe inkunga yubaka igihugu.

Agira imitsindo itsindira Urwanda
Kandi agatsinda yubaha ababyeyi.
Arahalira kukarubanda
Ko byanze bikunze, bitinde bitebuke
Urwanda ruzaba rutinwa.
Rukaba ikirangirire kwisi hose.

Ati : ntakizaruhangara mpahagaze
Nzatega abanzi imitsindo
 ihagatiwe nabarukunda.

Nzabatega ababyeyi barwambarira
impumbya ubudahwema,

Mbatege abo bategarugore
dore ko aribo baheka abatabazi,
Bahora barutegeye urugore ngo barwizihize.
Aho baba bari hose baba barufatiye iryibiryo
ngo rudahungabana.

Iyo mitsindo yabanyampinga
ibarohe ishyanga

Nibahagera mbagire ibiragi
Nibavuga bavugishwe
Bati baravuga aya Ndongo nindondogozi.

Nzabatega Rwema utambuka nka Rwanyonga
Uwo bareba bararamye
Kabareba Jamesi ntazatuma
barenga umutaru.

Nibatisubiraho ngo dufatanye kubaka urwacu
Bahere ishyanga bambaye isoni.
Dore ko ingabo zange zishinga
ikirenge mukingangurarugo.
zituma Urwanda ruba rutinwa
Bakaruhururira,
bakaruhuruza aho bicika baruririmba,
ngo bicube bagire amahoro nkayacu.

Aho amahanga ahurura baza i Rwanda
ngo hariyo Kagame
wambika abagome imigoma.
Bati turaje ngo utwigishe, uko
ubigenza ngo ube igihangange.

Bamugera imbere ati reka reka niko navutse.
Ati ibyo mureba ibi numurage
kandi byari bizwi ko bizagaruka
kuko Urwanda ruzwiho ubutwari budaheranwa.

Sinata umuco ngo ntatire umurage wubutwari

sinaba ikigwari narateganijwe
Ngo nzashyirwe kumurongo wingenzi mumateka
azasigare yigisha abazaza.
Bazaharanire kwiga aya
Rukaraga muheto rwa mudatinya.

Sinigeze mba ikigwari nkirumwana
Ninabyo byatumye ndahemuka mubuzima nanyuzemo

Rugira yanteganirije kuzaramira Urwanda
nkazaramiza amata abarutuye bagashira inyota
bakanyirahira bakanyita Kiramira.

Dore ko bagira bati
twamuboneye kwirembo
tumubonamo ko ariwe Rutinwa
uzaca ibirumbo Murwanda
ntituzongere kugira injajwa zitujujubya.

Cyane cyane abumururumba
binda ziteretse hejuru yimitima
Bashakira inzaratsi mumafaranga
Bakibagirwa ko
harubwo bibagira ingegera
bashaka kugamburuza Rugennyi
Ntaho byabaye.

Kagame abo iyababonye ababwira
ko babeshya kandi bibeshya
ati Urwanda kulimwe nzaruzengurutsa

Imbariro zimirinzi -urugo alimiyenzi
Urwo rugo ruzajja rwinjirwamo
nintwari zambaye umurava.
Imyugariro ibe insobe zubumwe twiyemeje.

KAGAME

I am an artist portraying facts
Let me tell you how I see President Kagame
What I am telling is no gossip
You will quickly notice that is the truth
His image is as hard as a rock
His eye scare his aggressors
He renders his foes' plots futile
It is him who defeats his rivals
When he is happy he smiles
And his smile so beautiful
But he hates all sorts of misdeeds
And hates those who advocate misdeeds
He does his best to educate them
Keeping them close to himself
He is always faultless
And natural born perfection

God made him a hero
And made him unassailable
He was given a knighthood
Recognition well deserved
He was made the caretaker of Rwanda and its people.
God made him hope for Rwanda and

Everyone who loves Rwanda
He hates whispering, mumbling and murmuring
Those voices not loud and clear
The low tone voices which do not help Rwanda
He has always led Rwanda to victory
Paying great respect to the elders
He swears publicly
That sooner or later
Rwanda shall be knighted
And will gain popularity all over the world

He says: Nothing will threaten Rwanda on my watch
I will defeat my enemies
Hand in hand with friends of Rwanda
They will be defeated by ongoing curses and prayers from
parents
They will face defeat from committed women
For it's them who breed my army
Ladies standing tall and alerted to put on victory parades
And on their knees praying hard for Rwanda to be secure

The curses of parents will lead them to hell
And once they are in hell they will turn deaf
But should they try to speak, they will stumble
I will set my hero who walks like Rwanyonga to block
them
Who they will need to look up to with their heads raised
James Kabarebe will halt all their moves
Should they not redeem themselves?
And be party to the reconstruction of our country

25

Let them stay in exile living with shame
The unprecedented superiority and discipline of my army
Makes Rwanda a frightening nation in the eyes of my
enemies
With the world at large turning to us for help and
protection
Hoping to enjoy peace like ours

Rwanda, where the world assembles
Assembling, trying to understand and learn Kagame's ways
Ways he insists that it's mother nature
His courage is partly a Rwandan heritage
History indeed repeats itself
Mighty Rwanda with extraordinary people
I am not willing to compromise my cultural heritage
I am not willing to be a villain
Because I was chosen to be part of my country's history
A history that will provide guidance to the generations to
come
So that the next generation shall learn from our experiences

I shall never be a villain
Nor do I want to look back with regrets
I am here with a purpose to fulfill
That purpose is to stand out tall whenever my country is
calling
To provide milk to my people so that no one starves
We shall walk together as a nation
The whole nation shouting my name as I emerge out as
their hero

When they saw him the very first time they knew
That he is the one who will clear our Rwanda from rubbish
of any kind.
Mostly those who are greedy.
Those who will never have enough.
Those who think that money is everything
And forget to love others and humanity
Who forget that time can come when their behaviour
Can throw them in the hole.
And think that they can get wherever they want when they
want it.
Who forget that they are God who is above all?
People like them Kagame when come across to them
He tells them that they are lying to themselves and to
others around them.
That he will build Rwanda a tight and strong fence to
Rwanda
Rwanda will be guided by Rwandan's culture, heritage of
bravery and love unity of Rwandans.
Nothing will shake Rwanda when I am still alive.

GENDA NKUBITO YIMANZI WALINGENZI

Amabyiruka yawe Rukabu yarabigaragaje
Ko Urwanda rukubyiruyeho ingirakamaro
Ukuyeho uburanga buteye ubwuzu
Nigihagararo giteye ishema
Rukabu warushije benchi ibitekerezo biteye imbere

Aho wagaragaje kenchi ko wanga ubusambo
Nibisambo byinda nini zitabumba
Abagendana izidahaga
Izobateretse hejuru yimitima
Ukanga abo biyo mitima
Yasinzilijwe nokunyaga namahugu

Aliko Rukabu uti nzabarwanya
Kuko nkunda Urwanda rwange
Uti benabo aho kubaka barasenya
Kandi Rukabu wahoraga urahira
Ko mwene Musinga batazagusenyana igihugu.
Uvutse wasanze Urwanda ali nyabagendwa
Usanga arurwakanyarwanda

Usanga ba Sogokuruza bararubumbatiye
Bararwagura barubumbira hamwe

Barwambika icyubahiro ruba ijabiro
Bakubwira Nsoro arutabaza ibyiwe byacitse
Ingangurarugo zikajja kubishyira mubiryo.
Icyogihe zishorewe na
Seruzamba rwa Kinani cya Birabonye.
Byatungana bati Tanzania yanyu ngiyo turatashye.
Ubwo hacyitwa mu Bushubi.

Nibindi nkibyo byaguteye ubutwali bugira bake
Uti sinzabera Urwanda ikigwali
Nzagaragaza ko intwali zivuka iteka
Nzasiga umurage uzaba karande
Nabazibeshya igihe kizagera bagire isoni.

Kuko nzahora ndi Rudahigwa ahakomeye
Aho nzaba ndi hose nzarangwa nubukaka
Abambonye bati nguwo Rukabu araje
Mbabere umubyeyi numutabazi
Nzabamara agahinda mbahe nubulinganire

Sinzaruhuka Africa itarava mubuja
Nzabanziliza kukarere kange
Nzavugana nabagenzi bange
Duhangane nabanzi dukura abacu mubuja
Tuzabarwanisha kubaka amashuli
Abana bakurire mubujijuke
Nzashaka Mutesa na Gasyonga
Mvugane na Mwambutsa na Rumumba
Tubereke ko hano aliwacu nomubacu

Ndumwana aliko ndareba
Nzafata ingero zaho mvuka
Zumurage wacu wubutwari

Ndibuka imihigo yokwagura Urwanda
Abashyitsi baje mbashinze ijisho
Mbona atarabashyitsi nkabasanzwe
Aba nibagatumwa aliko turareba
Baduteyemo imirwi batwita amazina
Batwambika ibyera ngo tulizihiwe
Aliko bo bazi ko baduculika

Aho mba mpagaze iyo duhagararanye
Aho bazararamira ngo bandebe mumaso
Rudahigwa jje mbanabarangije hose.

Babonye mbaphukamiye bacyeka ko bambonye
Banyurwa manuma ngo mbayuwabo
Naho napfukamye kuba Karoli
Ngo bimbere indorerwamo mbarunguruke
Dore ko amacenga yabo ankura umutima
Imbabazi zirusha izanyina wumwana
Ngo badukunze kurusha uko twikunda
Maze menye ibyabo mfate imigambi

Haciye kabili bacira Data ishyanga
Bamuziza ko yanze kubaha Urwanda
Abashenzi babona ko nabishimye
Bati ngwino Karoli wowe uru uwacu.

Ubwo ngo bazi ko ngiye kuba ikibambasi
Bakankinga bakica abange
Ngo sinkili Rudahigwa nabaye Karili
Rukabu nababwiye ko bibeshye
Nti ndacyali Rudahigwa wa Musinga
Iwacu kirazira ntiduhana abacu
Ahubwo turabitangira iyo bibaye ngombwa
Uwo numurage nasanze

Nzarwana kurwanda muburyo bwose
Aho kugirango ruzarohame mbireba
Nzarwitangire nibiba ngombwa
Murabizi ko munteze kenchi
Imitego nyisimbuka mubireba

Nubwo mwanjanye iwanyu narawurenze
Nkubitoyimanzi mugiye kubona mumbona Inyanza
Nti nimugenze buhoro Igihe nikigera, nzabizanira
Kuko ndi Rudahigwa, rudakurwa kwijambo
Nacyane iyalilirengera abange.

Nimubona mbizaniye muzatinye
Kuko bizaba biteguye ahakomeye
Icyonanze nakarengane mu Rwanda
Ibyo mutsindagira mushaka kubyitwaza
Ngo ubuhake nuburetwa kandi nibugumeho
Aliko jje kuko nchaka ubwisanzure bwanyabwo
Ataribyo mutubeshye mubyita democrasi
Umunyarwanda akorane nundi atitwa umuhakwa

Ayo niyo majjambere yukuri akwiye
Ndashaka ko dutera intambwe mubujijuke
Bitarubwo bujiji mushaka kuduhezamo.

Babashyitsi bagatumwa babibonye batyo
Bati ibintu nibibili uhitemo kimwe.
Kureka abanyarwanda bakaguma mubuhake
Cyanga tukwice amanwa ava turutware.

Rukabu ati murabeshya ubuhake ndabwanze
Abanyarwanda ntibavukiye ingoyi
Sinareka ngo mwimakaze amateshwa
Sinaba ntibindeba ndi Mutara
Sinaba igitsimbanyi ndi Rukabu
Kandi naravutse ngo nzabe urumuli
Sinshaka kubiba ibitotsi
abange batazasarura ingonera
Ndashaka kuzasiga inzira imbuto itazazima
Ndashaka kubatega umutego
Uzaruhura Urwanda umutima
Rukitsa umutima ugasubira mugitereko
Kandi nzatsinda umwijima byo nta shiti

Mbizanire kuko ndi Rudatinya
Nkubito Yimanzi nzaza mbizi
Nzasezera murukali nokubahungu
Mbasange hanze mubanze kujijwa
Mbamare ubwoba ntinaje mbizi
Nti nakera niko bigenda
Iyo inzuzi zerekanaga insinzi ko arubwitange

Byitwaga kunwa amata ugatanga
Ugahereza abejeje icyogihe kigeze

Nimunyica sinzaba mfuye nzaba ntabaye
Ikindi kandi nzaba ntanze
Mpaye abajeje inzuzi kuko bahali
Amaraso yange azaba icyuhagiro
Cyagihe nababwiye nikigera
Igihe cyahanuwe nabahanga bacu
Ko amaraso yange azaba intsinzi
y'Urwanda nabanyarwanda
Ariko akazasama abayahangaye

Nzababera inkoma rume
Mbabere umusemburo wubwitange
Byatinda byatebuka igihe kizaza
Rukabu nzabatega urubyiruko ruzaza alintarumikwa
Ruva aho ruzaba rubundiye rutabare
Baze bakomereze aho nagejereje
Ruzabanyanyagiramo rukabanyanyagiza
Rukabakura amata mukanwa rukabakoza isoni

Bazayaramiza ababo bashire inyota
Bazasugira bagasagamba
Bazaba Rutinwa babe ibirangirire
Bakenyeze Urwanda ubumwe
Rwitere urukundo
Ikizabaranga nukwanga
akarengane nagasuzuguro
nkibinanga.

Bambare icyubahiro gikwire Urwanda
Icyo gihe muzavuga muti
ngaba abahungu ba Nkubitoyimanzi
Abo yaduteze yatubwiraga naba.
Turareba bazanye nabashiki babo
bateye ikirenge mucye tuberereke tugende.

Uwarumwami w'Urwanda Mutara Rudahigwa wa III, yatabaliye Urwanda yitangira Abanyarwanda asanga ababiligi Bujumbura Iburundi azi neza ko bali bumwice, aliko asanga igihe cyokwitanga kigeze. Rukabu atanze byahungabanije akarere kose, Uburundi na Congo dore ko bari bamaze gufatana urunana kurwanira ubwigenge bwabo. Urwannda rwabaye mubwigunge kuva uwo munsi kugeza -aho Urubyiruko rwambukiye bakaza bitwa Inkotanyi -1-10-1990 bakarwana urugamba rubohoza Urwanda burundu.

Rudahigwa numwe muntwali zabanyarwanda tutazibagirwa.

RUDAHIGWA

Nkubitoyimanzi you were the best in many ways. You show that in your early age.

That Rwanda had you as its saviour. Apart from how handsome you were. With your height which had few Rukabu you had thoughts which had vision to build Rwanda.

When you show people many times that you hate greedy people. Who had big stomach – which can't ever be full? Whom you can think that they put their stomach on top of their hearts. And you hated people with that kind of heart. Which always they are in big sleep busy betraying their country.

And say that Rukabu you will fight them. Because you love your country Rwanda.

People like that, instead of building they break. When you judge first you see both sides. You believe in ideas but not to talk in backs of other people. Because that is original of hate for no reason. And I know that is one of which breaks up the country.

I stand with them in a careful way as Rukabu. Rukabu you always say that son of Musinga you will not let them break the country. And say that when you were born Rwanda was a peaceful country, for all Rwandans. Your great parents put it together.

And made Rwanda to be a respectable country. He knows stories like when Nsoro asked Rwanda for help. When his country was in trouble. Rwanda sends its soldiers (Ingangurarugo and others). Under their commander Seruzamba son of Kinani. When time came they give back their country Tanzania, and go home. At that time was Bushubi.

You said that you will keep its pride. So Rwanda can be respectable for ever. You had many which made you to be brave and a hero. You heard a story when Ankole's King invented Rwanda, Rwanda fight back and win them with their guns. You said that you will never be useless to Rwanda.

You will show that heroes are always born.

I will give good heritage to Rwandans who will be here for ever. Who will come after me will follow it. They will be who will think that they can take Rwanda for guaranteed. Time will come when they will be ashamed.

I will always be Rudahigwa in hard situation. Wherever I will be I will be known for my bravery. Everyone who will see me knows that Rukabu I am there. I will be their parent, I will sacrifice for my people when it will be needed.

I will give them their right, they will never be sad when I am there. I will not rest before Africa is out of dictators of colonialism. I will start with my areas. By talking with my neighbours. So that we can stand to our people to see that they will be free.

We will fight them by building schools for our children.

In that way they will grow up as understanding people. I will talk with Mutesa and Gasyonga. I will talk with Mwambutsa and Rumumba. We will show them that here are our soils with our people.

I am young but I see everything. I will get good examples from my parents. Examples of bravery. I will fight for the society in general. I remember what they did to make Rwanda to be wider. I see very clear our visitors.

They are not normal visitors as I used to see others. They have an agenda but we are together. They divided us and give us their names! They give us white dresses to make us look smart. But they know that they are putting us upside down. When I am standing, when I am with them, the time they still struggle to look at my face, within no time Rudahigwa I had finish to look at them from the head to toes.

When they saw that I kneeled to their gods. They were happy that they got me. And believed that I am theirs. Little they knew that I kneeled to be Karoli. So that can be my mirror to see them through. Their behaviour is scary.

Especially when they show us a lot of love, more than how we love ourselves! Want to know about them and then know what to do after. After short time they sent my father in exile. Just because he refused to give them his country.

The bastard thought that I am happy with it! And tell me that I don't have to to worry, I am theirs!

The believed that they are going to use me the way they want. So they can get an easy way to kill my people. That I am no longer Rudahigwa, I am changed to Karoli. I told them that they lied for themselves. I am still Rudahigwa Musinga's son.

I told them that in my culture are impossible. I have to fight for my people, I can be sacrificed for them when necessary.

That is our innate. I will fight for Rwanda in all means. Instead to wait and see when Rwanda is drowned. You know how many times you have tried to assassinate me. I was surprising you how I survived. Even when you took me to your country. With no time you saw me back home (Inyanza).

I told you to take it easy, that time will come. That time I will come by myself. Because I am Rudahigwa who can't change my mind from the truth to the rubbish. Especially when is side of help my people. At that time I will be happy to give myself to you. So that my blood can be cause of peace.

In that way I will leave behind good heritage of bravery. Instead of leaving uselessness, laziness, or nothing behind me. When that time will come. And see that I come, to give up to you by myself. Be aware that it will not be a joke.

What I want in Rwanda is freedom. What you insist is that domestic is not right, but have to be permanent with Rwandans, and here you call it democracy.

That is what I refused; I want Rwandans to work with each other, but not in servants system. That is true improvement and proper democracy. What I want is Rwandans to be ahead in life, not that way you are trying to drown us in deep primitive for ever.

When our abnormal visitors saw my plans, they told me that they two things I have to choose one. To let Rwandans die in domestic or to kill you in daylight and take Rwanda for themselves.

Rukabu told them that no way to sell my people and my country. Rwandans they are not born to be servants forever, I can't let you make rubbish point. I can't say that I am not responsible when I am Mutara. I can't be a coward when I am Rukabu.

I was born to be the light. I don't want to leave behind laziness to my people. So can't be inheritance to them. I want to leave good seeds for tomorrow for their future. I want to leave back secret which will save Rwanda.

So that can have back their peace and be happy in life. When you will kill me you will think that I died – but you will be made my seeds to grow quick and be strong. The seeds of peace, love and unity within Rwandans. The patriotic people don't die, what they leave behind grow and go ahead again, they born every day. They will be told my work which I didn't finish they will like it, and fight for it. When I will see that my seeds have got a way for tomorrow, I will come to give up myself to you, because I am Rukabu.

Nkubitoyimanzi, I will be aware when I will come. I will say bye to my people. When you will see me, first you will be confused. I will tell you that go ahead I am ready. That is one of our cultures, when time comes for sacrifices for our people. We have a name of it – that is (GUTANGA), to give others and go in brave way.

To give the one who will come for the right time, my blood will be blessings to them and their country, but will be a curse to them, who will not respect it. I will be with them everywhere. I will be spices for their work – sooner or later, time will come. Rukabu, I have a secret of young people who will see that they are capable. Will come from where they will be and come to save their country.

Their high morale will shock you. They will start their work from where I will leave it. They will come with determination which will take you everywhere looking for survival. Will shame you, will be hungry and thirsty, when they will give their people enough milk to be no thirstier, no more suffering. They will have more children and become strong families and strong. They will have respect around the world.

Rwandans will have their lives back and unity again. How you will know that is them they will fight for the right and they will not like ignorance like me now. They will be respected and fearfully with others around them. At that time know that is them I was telling you, my sons with their sisters.

Can't stand this heroism, let us go, our time is over.

That was Rwandan King MUTARA RUDAHIGWA III. He was sacrificed for Rwandans and his country, when he went to meet Belgians in BUJUMBURA Burundi he was aware that they would kill him, but saw that it was time. After that was the beginning of trouble in the whole area, Burundi, Congo, as all of them were planning to fight for their freedom, Rwanda was in big upside down from then until when R P F came to rescue the country in 1990 and fight to give Rwandans the freedom they deserve.

Rudahigwa is one of Rwandan heroes who can't ever be forgotten by Rwandans.

INKOTA YINDA

Ndimbugita yicyatwa
Yicyamamare kwisihose
Abakuru nabato barandilimba
Nomunyamaswa imihigo yange irahaganje
Alimunyanja nokubutayu.
Inkota yange ntaho idafite icyate.

Dore ko igihumeka cyindamya cyikivuka
Cyigatabaza cyiti nimutabare itarancha ijosi
Ndasogota
Nkanyanyagiza
Ngasandaza
Ikamba ryange ni Rusoferi.

Ubwema bwange bukandagira hose
Munzego zose ningano zose
Ntampuhwe ntambabazi
mba ndwana kungoma yange.
Ngira gifasha ingabo yange nimwe rukumbi.

Nayitoranije nashishoje
Mbanza kugira impungenge ko bazayihunga
Yenda bavumbuye imigimbi yayo

Bashishoje bakitegereza ikirezi inigilije.
Dore ko umudende wayo akenchi aligihanga.

Icyo cyirezi cyayo nïrugamburuza
Gishashagirana nki inyenyeri
Giteye ubwuzu iyukireba
Ukaba wakwifuza nokucyirunguruka
Nubwo utagishyikira ngo kibe hafi

Ubwo ugakubita urutoke kurundi
Uti yenda ejo nzagushyikira
Nkwiyegereze hose
Ubwo bwiza bwawe bunsesekareho
Kuva kumutwe nokubirenge

Nguhobere nkwereke urukundo
Nkwigaragureho ndetse nakwisasire
Ngusenge umpeke unjane ahonja hose.

Urigase icyo cyirezi akabyita umugisha
Akaba asogongeye uburyohe bwacyo
Agasanga cyiryoshye kurushya umutobe
Ati byanze bikunze nzakwiruka inyuma nzagutunge.

Ubwo nange nkaba nakubonye
Ntingwino niwowe nalintegereje
Uwo nteye imbone nkuwo simfafate icyate,
Ahubwo jje mufataho igikingi.
Byaba mahire ngasanga ntabuphura
Ubwo nkagura inda nkamwiba umutima

Kuko mbanza kuyungurura
Inyangamugayo zindahemuka
Nabona uzangora nkamuha ibye nkagenda

Ubwo ngashaka uwo nzegukana
Namubona nkamwibasira
Mubwirwa nuko ankanga ngo ninyangamugayo
Kandi jje namuteye imbone
Nti nayubusa nzakujjana
Kukodinkabakozi bose
Mbe nkabatumwa gushaka abayoboke
Nange mbanchaka kugira benchi.

Ngaharanira kutaneshwa ngo ndeke ejo uzananire
Ugume mumubare muto winyangamugayo
Nti reka bagumye babe inkeho nzakujjana.
Nibiba ngombwa nzagusogongeza.
Unkulikire aruko umenye uko ndryoshye

Aho nzakugira umugaragu wange.
Ningira amahirwe uzabe imbata
Ninguhaga nzakurekura mfate abandi
Ubwo usigare ubunga ubunza imitima
Ntakikujjanye.
Dore ko akenchi abo njugunye mbajugunya nabi
Nokwa Nyangamugayo baguhunge
Ubure amajjo, ubara ibyahise, byabaye ibyabandi.
Uti nange kera nari nkanaka.

Icyo gihe bati umva ngo ararata inkovu zimilinga

Ndi ntabikangwa uwansogongeye nibake banyikura
Nibake tubana simbahindure ingeso
Ngo mbace kunchuti zabo zimbata
Ndetse iyo nchatse mbigisha ingendo
Byaba ngombwa agahindura imvugo
akaniga amajwi uwo bahuye akamenya ko namujjanye

Ndinkozi yamahano ntampuhwe ntasoni nigeze
Ntibabeshye ngira icyonfana na Rusoferi
Sintinya nimiryango kuyicagagura
Nkayisandaza nkasiga aribishwange
Ndi intabikangwa nigerera nababyeyi
Nkabamenesha amabanga bagahemuka.
Cyanga abana bati ntuzongere kumbyara
Hahirwa unchikira akananira
Akantunga mubwitonzi
Agakomera kumurava nubunyangamugayo
Uwo usanga bamwifuza.

Nahubundi jje iyo nitumye igihugu bwo
Dore ko ngira amacenga
Abagituye babamo ukubili
Abo nemereye guhaka bakandilimba
Bakemera ko bavukanye amahirwe
Kubera ubwo bwiza bundanga
Cyagihugu kubwamakuba
Bagatangira kunchuranwa.

Ubundi nkababashyiramo amacenga
Dore ko nayagiriye mumashuli

Hakaba ubwo mbyanga bakamarana.
Ubwo igihugu cyikaba cyiroramye
Ahongaramye nkikora muntoke
Nti burya banyirukira bataramenya
Batabanje kwiha umwanya ngo bashishoze
Ngo bamenye ko nahagurukijwe nokuyungurura.
Ndetse nokulimbura
Abo bavukanye izadahaga
Bakaba intabikangwa nobwo bamara ababo
Aliko bakanigiriza icyo kirezi cyange.
Hakaba abandi banze kuba ingwate zange
Ahubwo bakamirwa barora.
Bakumirwa bakiyemeza
Bati ayubusa ntituzaba mpemuke ndamuke.

Nahalintwaro zadutse zubu
Inkota yange ntihakangwa
Nitwaje yangabo yange imwe rukumbi
IYO BISE IFARANGA
ABANDI BAKAYITA AMAHERA
Ngo kuko azamira ubuphura bugahera buheze.

IINKOTA IN ENGLISH
(SWORD)

I am a sharp knife
Well known worldwide
The elderly and youth praise me
Even among animals my plan is on top
In lakes and shores
My sword has a place everywhere
Every live creature praises me at birth
It calls for help before I cut through its throat
I pierce, break up
Scatter.
My crown is Lucifer.
My fame leads me all around
Among all classes and levels
No pity or mercy
I always protect my kingdom.
I have a helper who can't ever fail.
This is only one.
I selected it after research.
I was anxious to be ignored
Maybe after discovering its purpose
After discovering its origin…
Its major characteristic is wisdom…

Its characteristic is division
It twinkles like a star
It brings joy when you look at it
You just wish to lean over and look at it.
Even if you don't get closer
There you celebrate
You get hope that you will get closer next day.
I will get you closer
Your beauty shall shower on me.
I will hug you and shower you with my love
Shall roll on you and make you my bedding
Request you to carry me on your back and take me everywhere
    you go
Anyone who tastes you it's sweeter than honey
By all means I will chase and own you
I have also got you
I have been waiting for you
Then one I have infected…
I just make him my pillar
When I am just lucky and land on the disrespectful
I just buy his stomach and steal his heart
I first filter.
The honest and respectful
When I sense stubborn ones
I give them their share and go away.
I continue to look for one I will take for good
When I get one I carry him and tell him not to scare me with
    his honesty
When I give him bait
All the same I will take you.

I am like other workers
I am like a disciple looking for smart ones.
I also want many followers
I struggle not to be overpowered
You should remain in the few honest ones.
Let them be… I will take you if necessary I will give you a
    taste
You follow me known, after realising how sweet I am.
I will make you my slave
When I am lucky you will become my senior slave
When I get fed up I will drop you and get others
You will get unsettled and confused
Gone for nothing
I drop many in a desperate manner
Gone for nothing
I drop many in a desperate manner
The honest shall ignore you
You will lose connection
Counting the past
Which belong to others?
That I was once among the rich
They will mock you that you show off scars
I am terrible, anyone who tasted me does not ignore me
Very few stay with me and remain the same
I separate them from their friends
Sometimes they change their way of talking
He can change voices and others will know I have taken over.
I am criminal, without pity and I am not ashamed
It is not a lie, I am related to Lucifer
I do not fear separating families

I scatter them into pieces
I am not threatened. I even attack the parents
I make them reveal secrets and become unfaithful
Their children denounce them as parents
The lucky ones are those who escape from me
You own me with humbleness
Strong with determination and honesty
You will be liked
If I attack a country
I have many tactics.
The citizens divide themselves into two or more
Those under my governance praise me
They believe that they were born lucky
Because of my beauty that defines me
This country, unfortunately
They are covered with greed
Sometimes I give them more tactics
I am a professional tactician
I sometimes ignore them and see how they finish each other
Here the country shall be lost
From my watch point, I congratulate myself!
Oh! They rush to me before knowing who I am
Before they take time to research about me
In addition to uproot
Those who were born with greed
Even if it means to become unthreatened and kill and kill
    their people
And they continue to praise my character
They are some who refused to become my followers
They are instead swallowed alive

They also wonder and boast
Whatever it will be we will never be yours
Even where there are the latest weapons
My sword shall not fear
I move with my only one my usual sword of survival
Which is named MONEY.
They are who call it AMAHERA.
Because sometimes it can swallow respect, honour, to
disappear forever.

UMUCO NIKI?

Umuco numwambaro wizihira nyirawo,
Ugira amahirwe arawitera
Ninkingi ishorera ubumwe, urukondo, ishyaka nubutwali.
Bikamuranga aho anyuze hose
Ukamuha ijambo ukamuha icyicaro.
Babimubonamo nyirawo bakabimwubahira.
Maze agatsinda niwe ubibanza,
Akubaha abandi akaba umwigisha.

Umuco nindanga muntu, nyirawo haraho batamenya uko
    yitwa.
Ugasanga bamusobanura mumyifatireye.
Bati ese uravuga wawundi wimico myiza?
Wawundi wubaha akanafasha imbabare.
Bati niba aruwo turamuzi, icyingenzi cyinamuranga
Nuko akize cyane aliko akaba atirata.

Kandi uriya yigeze nogucyena, jje warumuzi mulibyo bihe
Acyernye cyane ntiyigunze
Ngo atinye abandi abure ijambo.
Ngo yihebe bimutere guhemuka.
Kuriwe imibereho yose ntimukanga
Ngo ate umuco kubera ibyo bihe.

Arareka ibihe akaba aribyo binyeganyega
Bigahinduka uko bishaka.
Dore ko nubusangwe bavuga ko
imfura irikira ntiiyirate, yanakena ntihemuke.

Uyumushinga uri iwacu witerambere.
Numushinga udasubira inyuma.
Mumyaka yimbere nka 50 nambere yaho.
Urwanda ruzaba arurundi.
Urwubu barureba mubitabo.

Yemwe bana, ndabasaba ngo MUNYUMVE.
Burya kugenda bitera kubona.
Mwirinde guhemukira abejo
Mwibura umwanya wokwegera abakuru
Nimukunde umuco nyarwanda utunga nyirawo.

Ejo batazasanga
Ibyiswe imico kandi atarimico.
Ibyari bibi bikitwa byiza, ibyari byiza bikitwa bibi
Umwijuto wabateye gusingiza ifaranga.
Batavaho bananirwa kurera abo babyaye
Bakabareresha mubandi
Bagakura buphubyi
Bagahinduka ibyigenge
Aho usanga abagore basheze ngo bahunduke abagabo!
Abagabo nabo baharanira guhinduka abagore!
Ngo bajijutse kandi bazi uburenganzi bwabo.

Bati nimureke umugabo arongora umugabo

Umugore nawe arongora umugore.

Ntihagire uwubahirwa ko akuze.
Umukuru nawe ntiyubahe abaruta ngo abahe urwo rugero
Mbe bicurikirana bivange vange rubure gica.

Mukomere kumuco Nyarwanda
Kuko umuryango utagira umuco uracika
Igihugu cyitawufite cyikorama
Uwufite umutera ubwema akagira igikundiro
Agatera ubwuzu abamuri hafi, bakamusobanuza aho akomoka.
Uwo ahabwiye akahakunda aribwo akihumva.

Mumenye ko imico nyarwanda ari nkigihango
Idatatirwa arumurage.
Kandi imico yiwacu igira uko yitwa.
Abakurambere bayise Imico KARANDE.

WHAT IS CULTURAL NORM?

Cultural normal is dressing that fits the owner
The luck one wears it
Is the pillar of unity, happiness, love, zeal and courage?
It identifies him or her wherever he or she go
It gives the person speech and platform
It is identified in the owner and is respected
He or she finally leads and succeeds
Respect others and become their teacher
Cultural norm is a personal identity; others might not even
    know your name
They will describe you in regard to your conduct
Eh do you mean that person with good conduct
That one who is extraordinarily respectful
Yes, we know him or her due to his or her good conduct
He or she is rich but do not boast.
He or she has even been poor.
During poverty periods, he or she did not isolate himself or
    herself.
Did not lose hope to become shameful.
He or she is not scared of anything.
Does not drop the norm due to changing situations
He or she lets a situation shake itself.

And changes as they wish.

They are saying that gentleman neither boasts when he is rich, nor when he is poor

This is our pillar for development

This program of AGACIRO is not backwards.

In 50 years or before from today

Rwanda will be a different country

The present Rwanda will be history published in the books.

He children.

Listen to me

When you travel you see different things.

Avoid disappointments the future generation

Do not fail to spare time for discussing with the elders.

And you parents do not fail to get time for your children.

Love a Rwandan cultural norm which supports its natives

Future generations should not find the so called norms, not the real ones

What was bad being called good, and good called bad?

Greed led to Praise Money

They fail to nurture their children

They are nurtured by others

They grow like orphans

They turn rebellious

Perform atrocities

They lack friendship and are neglected

They are left in friendship of **dogs** and **TV**.

Women will spearhead to become men!

When men will also spearhead to become women!

That they are educated and have equal rights!

Let a man marry a man!

And women marry a woman!
When no one will be respected for age
The elderly shall not respect the young
To lead as an example
They will be a mixed-up and have no solution.
Stick to Rwandan cultural norm
Know where you begin and end
The family without a norm breaks.
A country without a norm fails
The cultural norm of Rwandans to live together and help
each other.
One with it is full of happiness and love
He becomes a concern to neighbours who ask him about
his/her origin
The one he/she tells about it immediately loves it even it's
the first time they hear Rwanda.
Know that Rwanda norms are like a covenant
It is not force but a must
Our cultural norms have an identity
The fore fathers called it LONG LIFE CULTURAL
NORMS.

INAMA YUBUTABAZI

Abana bati igihe kirageze
Imyaka ibaye myinchi
Ntidutegereze ngo haze iyindi
Dufate umuheto kuko bibaye ngombwa.
Rudatinya ahakomeye Rwigema Gisa Fred.
Na Kagame Paul bati nimuze twuzuze inama yubutabazi.
Bati ubu inkunga yacu igize akamaro Mozambiqe na Uganda
Rwigema ati umugore wigize igihinza mumajjaruguru ya
    Uganda
Niwe uzibyange azababwira
Ahonamushushubikanyaga
Muroha muli Kenya
Rakwena kugeza nubu yangize indahiro.

Nkunda isi yose aliko byumwahiliko nkunda Afrika.
Kuko nubusangwe utanga uburezi abwibanza.
Nicyo gituma nanze kuzagwa ishyanga.
Kandi Urwanda rumbyiruyeho intwali
Nkaterwa agahinda nuko mbyirukiye hanze
Nti ejo ntazavaho alinaho nsiga ubuzima bwange

Kandi ngifite inchingano zatumye mvuka.
Ngo nzatabaruke nageze iwacu.
Amaraso yange aliho nyasheshe

yaba umusemburo wamahirwe yabange
Ngasiga mpateye imbuto izaba karande.
Sindigenyine mfite abo twabyirukanye
Barambiwe kuba ishyanga.
Kandi niwacu ntaburinganire abahari barababaye

Nitubishyira iburyo turahamagara abahungu
Ndetse nabashiki bacu badakorwa mujisho
Maze tunononsora inama yubutabazi.

Bibaye ngombwa ngo duhindure umuheto.
Tuwerekeze kuli Kinani kuko yigize ikiragi
Atinyutse kutubwira ko Urwanda rwuzuye
ngo nkikirahure cyuzuye amazi ntitwahakwirwa!
Kandi byanze bikunze tuzahakwirwa
Yiyibagije ko aho umwaga utari uruhu
rwisasira batanu.
Cyanga ko ntamubyeyi unanirwa ikibondo
Yanze kutwumva kuneza
Akitwita inyenzi dore ko yaba akeka ko tucyiri zazindi
Akibagirwa ko turi abubu.
Ntanashishwa akanatwita Inyangarwanda!

Abana bashegeshwe nogukurira imahanga
Agahinda twakuranye kaduteye ubutwari
Ikindi turi kwisi hose, nomubirwa bya Pacific
turahali, ahohose twahashye ubuhanga

Nidukoma imbarutso impuruza yacu izagera kure
Abasore kwisi hose bazafata umuheto

Nabo mu Rwanda bucece bazatuvuna.
Ababyeyi bacu bazasigara.
Aliko inyuma aho bali bazadufasha
Bose abacu inyuma, inkunga yabo bazayimenya
Twabanye neza ninshuti zacu nazo zizatavuna.
Inama yubutabazi igihe cyayo cyirageze

Kagame Paul ati reka nsige inyuma Rwigema nje kwiga
Ndamwizeye nicyo gituma ngiye
Nibiba ngombwa nzabavuna
Nzaza vuba kuko nzaguruka
Icyo mbijeje nuko nimpagera
Urwanda rwacu ruzaba intanga rugero
Nzarubera igiti cyumuzabibu
Nzashibure amashami yamahoro hirya hino
Abanyarwanda banwe divai
Igihugu cyose gishire inyota
Nzaba ndigiti kinganzamarumbo
Kidahungabanwa nimiyaga
Abakunda amahoro banyegere
Amahanga ahuruzwe nokwiga ibyizontwari
Iyinama yacu iziye kugihe.
Ndayishyigikiye.

Rutaremara Tito na Mazimpaka Patrick
Bati nimuhumure tubali hafi
Tuzababera abajjanama badahuga
Tubahugure hose aho muli.
Kandi twitonde mubushishozi
Byanze bikunze dutsinde abanzi

Inama yubutabazi turayishyigikiye

Mugambage Frank na Kayizare Ceasar
Bati tulikumwe na Rutatina Eugen
Ntaho tuzatinya, ntawe tuzatinya
Imyaka ibaye myinchi tutazwi
None reka tujje ahagaraga baturebe
Ntakizaduhagarara imbere ubu turagiye
Iki nigihe cyokubyuka turaje
Inama yubutabazi turayishyigikiye

Ndushabandi balikumwe na Mutimbo
bati twe turabaganga
Reka tugende tuzabavura
Aho imiti izava biratureba
Ikiza burya tuli kwisi hose
Inama yubutabazi turayishyigikiye

Kabarebe Gemes ati burya polotiq yubuke ntijja inkanga
Ikinkanga nubuke bwibitekerezo
Tuzagenda tulingangurarugo
Nzaba ndi I Rwanda kandi ndi Congo
Nzashinge iteka muli Africa nkumunyarwanda
Nyobore ingabo zibihugu bibili mugihe kimwe
Kuko ubu byanze bikunze turatabaye

Ati sinategereza kuzongera kubwirwa ko hirya hino nanzwe
Iryo nabwiwe rikantera agahinda numujinya wubutwali
Iryatumye nsanga Museveni mwishyamba

Sinazarira ejo umwana wange atazalibwirwa
None inama yubutabazi ndayishyigikiye

Nzaramba Martin bati wowe ubwo witonda
Uzakoreshe siasa yabongereza
Ubundi ngo niyo dipromas
Kubwira neza umwanzi usanze
Ntavumbure ko umucenga
Bigatuma yibagirwa akasamanga
Ugafata ibyemezo uvuga uti ngufashe mpili.
Ahasigaye inama yubutabazi tuyikomereho

Kaka Sam ati iyonama ndayishyigikiye
Reka tuzatahe ubudasubira inyuma
Byibura abacu batinyuke kwitwa Mutabazi na Nyampinga
Katende na Namatovu tujje tuyasura.

Karenzi Karacye na Nyamvumba bati siyasa yacu niyubwira
Ntidushaka kuzatinda tucyitwa inyeshyamba
Ntidushaka ko urwacu ruzaba nkorwa Angola cyanga muli
    Sudani
Turaashaka ko ibyacu bitungana bidatinze
Kuko intego yacu arukubona Afrika yose ituje tukava mubuja
    burundu
Ndetse dutware urugero rwibyacu muri Sudan.

Kayiteesi Doline na Roze Kanyange babwira Inyumba.
Bati iyinama tuyivuzeho iki
Bazana abandi bakobwa bajja hamwe
Bati nibyo tulibato kandi beza

Aliko ntitwigeze duteta kuko ntaho dutetera
Benchi hano turabali kandi iwacu baradukunze
Ukuyeho ko natwe tutiyanze
Basaza bacu ntibambuka bonyine twaronse limwe
Nimiruho twanyuzemo twarikumwe
Turambukana tubakubite ingabo mubitugu

Ntiturushanwa nabo mumbaraga zamaboko
Igikora nimbaraga zomumutwe turazifite
Nubwihangane bwumutima kamere muntu
Kandi ibihe byubu dukoresha mashini.

Sinkibya Ndabaga byarimiheto gakondo
Turashinga ikirenge mucye, aliko twe ntitwigira abahungu
Mureke dutabare turabakobwa.
Aho tuzaba tulihose, basaza bacu tubabe hafi
Kandi tubabereye Nyampinga
Inama yubutabazi turayishyigikiye

Reka tugende tucyure abandi bana
Bazige bamenyubwenge
Amanota yabo ajje aba ayabo
Ataribyi I Burundi bagenerwage ayabo
Cyanga I Rwanda kubwa Kinani
Ntibazabuzwa kwinjira Kaminuza
Nko muri Kenya UN ningabo zabo babimira.
Ngo kaminuza sizizimpunzi
Aliko ubwo umwana azajja yiga
Kuba alinde cyanga alinde
Bitamukura umutima ngo atinye.

Rose Kanyange bati wowe ufite ikibondo
Reka tugende urere uruhinja
Ati uwomwana arasigara ngende
Kuko nchaka kuzamurerera i Rwanda
Ikindi ndashaka kuzahangana numufaransa
Harukuntu akeka ko kuba umwirabura
Bisobanura kutagira umutima nkawe
Ndagirango nzababere ishuli
Mbakure mubitotsi bangire indahiro.

Bizabatere kubaha umwirabura hose aho bamusanze
Bati burya abirabura nabo nabantu

Bati ahubwo ducishe make bitadukoza isoni

Inama yubutabazi ndayishyigigikiye
Kandi ndambutse ndagiye

GAHONZIRE Mary ati ndahali
Jje nzajja mbamenyera hirya hino
Hatazagira ikizaza bucece kikabakanga
Hatazagira ikizabahungabanya
Nzakoresha ubuhanga ubwo mfite bwose
Ubwamashuli, uburere nubuvuke
Kandi mukazi ndumuhanga
Umunyarwandakazi azabe intanga rugero
Murwamubyaye nomumahanga.
Inama yubutabazi ndayishyigikiye.

Aho yaliyicaye Kayitare Emmanuel ati byose nabyumvise

Ibyinama yubutabazi ndikumwe namwe
Igihe cyokubabwira ibanga nicyi
Jje nali nalimenye nkirumwana
Kandi nabibwiwe nabambyaye
Ko ndumwe mubahanuwe bataravuka

Bati umunsi urwanda ruzagera ahaga
Hazaduka intwari imeze nka Ruganzu
Izarwitangira rukava ibuzimu rukajja ibumuntu
Ishusho yarwo igatangaza amahanga.
Abahanuzi bati icyogihe cyange.
Nzaba igitambo nzabe insinzi yabange.
Kumunsi bazahura nabasazi bambaye amashara.
Biyuhagiye amaraso
Igihe kizaba cyiegeze
Cyuko Urwanda rutemba amata rwaziganilijwe na Rurema
None nimuhaguruke dutabare igihe kirageze

Jje mpisemo ko muzamparira Uruhengeli nu Murera
Nzatsinda butwari icyo gihe nzaba mfite nizina ryubwema.
Nzaba naramaze kubatizwa ko ndi Intare batinya.

Nkusi Sam ati nzaza mbereke ubuhanga nahashye ibuzungu
Nimuhumure nzahanga radio Muhabura
Izahangane nizabanzi bibajijishe
Ihabure abacu bakore bugenge bitangaze
Bati ibyababana ntibisanzwe tubitege amaso
Bibulirwe izina bati ibi nibyo bita ubutatu butagatifu.
Iyonama yubutabazi ndayishyigikiye

Rusagara Franc ati iyonama ndayishyigikiye
Nange maze iminsi ndota Urwanda
Ngo ndikurugamba ndwana inkundura
Bati uyumusore wambariye urugamba
Unatera intambwe nka Nyiringango, yambaye insinzi
Kandi nkarota nganje natsinze abagome
Ngobabaririza abo turibo tarangwa nubutwari
Turakuze reka dutabalire Urwanda

Nziza Jack ati ntimunsiga turajjana
Burya kuba umufumbira bisobanura ubunyarwanda
Amateka yacu ntadutera isoni
Imipaka yaje ejubundi ntimuyishinge
Ejo ntazatinya intango yintwari ntalikigwali.
Inama yubutabazi ndayishyigikiye

Kayonga Charles ati nibyo tugende
Muzareke mbanze kumurwa i Kigali
Nzaba mbareba batandeba
Kubera ubuhanga nzaba njanye
Bankekere kumibare mbabwiye bahere kuliyo
Ahakomeye sinzahatinya
Nzashishoza ntegure amayira
Mubwitonzi nubwitange ducyure abacu.
Iyinama yubutabazi ndayishyigikiye

Mbandahe Mbayire Alfonci bimugezeho
Ati iyo niyonama yalitegerejwe
Hashize imyaka twitwa Inyenzi
Ubundi twiyoberanya ngo bucye kabiri.

Nimuze tureke ayomanyamaswa
Tuzahabwe ayubwema adukwiye
Tuzabayobora amayira mazima
Ayo mubishanga numubigunda
Maze tugote abagome tubatsinde
Umunyarwanda wese mu Rwanda
Abe we ntamushyitsi
Inama yubutabazi turayishyigikiye

Ba Kadogo bati twabyumvise
Ntimudusiga nubwo mutubuza
Tuzihisha tuze mubone tulikumwe
Ntako mukibigize mureke tuhagume
Maze twiyoberanye ngo turabana
Tugire akamaro mutangare

Abanyeshuli basize amakaramu kumeza
Abo mumajjaruguru ya Uganda barahindukira
Abaganga basiga amakote mubyumba
Abalimu nabo mubiro biha ibiruhuko
Ababyeyi bamwe barasezerwa,
Abana bati mwemere mwange Umusindi yarenze akarwa.
Zere zirabure turagiye
Ahubwo mwitungurwa igihe cyirageze.
Nimwahe impumbya,mudufatire iryiburyo turatabaye.

INAMA YUBUTABAZI

Intwari zatabaliye Urwanda mugihe cya 1990, abikubitiro
    bambutse 1-10-1990, nibenchi, baturutse impande zose

kwisi, bazanye ubuhanga butandukanye, arabatabarutse tulikumwe nabo, harinabatanze ubuzima bwabo tukaba tutalikumwe, aliko twarabasigaranye mumitima yacu. Arabakobwa arabahungu, sinavuze amazina yabose. Amazina avuzwe aha ahagarariye ayabandi.

Izo ntwari zacu zitazibagirana nizo dukesha Urwanda rwubu, tutibagirwa ababyeyi babo,abavandimwe, hamwe ninchuti, balinyuma yabo, babafasha kururwo rugamba, batanze inkunga zabo muburyo butandukanye, batanze imyanya yabo nibintu, batanze amatunga namafaranga, kugirango abafashe umuheto babishobore. Nabogushima. Bituma tugira ishema hose aho tunyuze, tukishimira ko turabanyarwanda.

LIBERATION LAUNCH

Children said, time is up.
Too many years have come to pass
We should not wait for more years
Let us get arms as it has become a must
Brave Rwigema Gisa Fred and
Kagame Paul said let us unite and build the liberation team
Now that our cause is supported by Mozambique and Uganda
Rwigema said that a woman rebels in Northern Uganda
She knows me and will tell you more
It gave her hard time, chased her from place to place
Dumped her into Kenya
Lakwena up now swears my name
I love the world but especially Africa because it is the pearl
    and beginning
That is why I cannot die in foreign land
Yet Rwanda has raised warriors
I feel sad that I am raised from foreign land
I have a fear that I might die in foreign land too
Yet I have a purpose of being born
I will rest when I reach home
My blood shed at my home country
This might be blessing to my country men and women
Planting a seed which will widely grow

I am not alone but with others together we grew
They are all tired of living as foreigners
At home there is no democracy,
After we have laid our work plan,
Even our sisters shall not be left out
Here was launched a liberation meeting.
It is necessary to change the direction for arms
Direct the arms towards the dictator with deaf ears
Without fear he told us that Rwanda is full
That like a glass full of water, we cannot be accommodated
But through all ways we shall be accommodated
Forgetting that where there is a will, there is a way,
Also no mother fails to look after her baby
He refused to listen peacefully
He still call us rebels expecting us to be the previous ones
Forgetting that we are modern
Without sensitivity he calls us rebels
That we didn't deserve Rwanda!
Children groomed and raised in foreign land
Grew in sorrow which gave us courage
We are scattered all over the world, including the Pacific
We are all over the world and we are educated
Once we hold the trigger, our case shall move faster
Boys and girls all over the world shall get arms
Those in Rwanda will secretly support us
Our parents shall stay behind
But behind them, shall get support
All our people shall know their contribution
We have lived in harmony, have been our good friends
Liberation Launch! Time is up

Kagame Paul said let me leave Rwigema and go for further
    studies.
I trust him, that is why I have to go.
Where there is urgency, I will burden you
I will come back soon, as soon as I will know I will fly.
I assure you when I reach my home country
Our Rwanda will be its olive tree
I will grow wide branches of peace side by side
Rwandans will drink wine
The whole country shall quench its thirst
I will be a tree which can't be shaken.
A firm tree which is not easily shaken by any wind
Those who love peace shall come to study and consult about
    the fighters
Our Liberation Launch has come at the right time.
I support it.
Rutaremara Tito and Mazimpaka Patrick
Do not worry, we are close to you
We shall be your genuine advisors
We shall advise you wherever you go
We shall be careful with secret investigations
By all means we shall overcome the enemies
Liberation Launch we support you.
Mugambage Frank and Kayizare Caesar
We are together with Rutatina Eugene
We shall not fear any place or one
For many years, we have not been in limelight
Let us go in limelight and they see us
Nothing will stop us, we are set to go
This is time to wake up! We have come

Liberation Launch! We support it.
Ndushabandi and Mutimbo
We, we are doctors
Let go us, we will support you
Regards all medicines, we shall be responsible.
Fortunately it's true we are all around the world.
Liberation Launch! We support you.
Kabarebe James, I am not scared of cheap politics
I am scared of cheap ideas
We shall go as liberators
I will be in Rwanda at the same time in Congo
I will reinstate policy in Africa as a Rwandan. I will lead
    fighters of two countries at the same time
By all means we have gone to battle.
I will not be reminded that I am not wanted
The word that angered me and filled with courage
It drove me to meet Museveni in the bush
I would not cry, if my child should not be told the same
Liberation Launch! I support you.
Nzaramba Martin, do not we are together.
Hard times train
Growing in foreign land grooms you to be wise
Let us cross the border, we shall overcome by all means
We have lawyers, we shall apply science.
And since I have few words
I will apply British science
That is diplomacy
Sweet talk the enemy you meet
Not giving him/her chance to suspect you
To an extent of forgetting and let out all secrets

Get exhibits and capture him
The rest, Liberation Launch! I support you.
Kaka Sam, Liberation Launch I support it
Let us return with no turning back.
At least our children shall be named Mutabazi and
Nyampinga
Katende and Namatovu shall be visited.
Liberation Launch, I support it.
Karenzi Karake and Nyamvumba, our science is anxiety
We do not want to continue being called rebels
We don't want our struggle to be like Angola's or Sudan's
We want ours to succeed without any delay
Our plan is to see Africa at peace out of slavery
We shall be a role model to Sudan.
Kayitesi Doreen and Inyumba Aloysia asked Rose Kanyange
What do we say about the Liberation Launch?
All of them at once said that they support it.
Yeah, we are still young and beautiful
But we have never been naughty, no conducive place
Many of us are here and were dearly loved at our home
country
We have not hated ourselves as well
Our brothers shall not go to the battlefield alone
We have shared all hardships
We shall cross the border together and support them.
We shall not compete physically
What is needed is mental power, which we have
Patience and personal determination.
This is a modern era, we use machine guns
Not like old days of arrows

We shall follow their steps, we shall not become boys.
Like Ndabaga we will only follow her braveness
Let us go to the battlefield, as girls!
Always we shall be near our brothers
And we shall be their immediate saviour
Liberation Launch we support it.
Let us go and liberate other children
They will study and become professionals
Their grades at schools will belong to them
Not as in Burundi where they had limited grades
Or in Rwanda during the days of dictators
They shall not be barred from joining University
Like in Kenya where the UN with their allies limited grades
Not even like in Uganda where you have to change the
    name.
But now a child will go to school
Despite the status of the child
Children shall be confident and shall not be scared.
Rose Kanyange you have a little baby
Let us go, you will look after the baby
The child will remain behind and I go
Because I want to raise him in Rwanda
I also want to face the French man
There is a way he thinks being black means not having
    natural feelings like him.
I want to be their lesson
I will wake them up
It will cause them to respect black people wherever they are.
Wake up and realise that black people are also human
They will change their attitude and feel ashamed

Liberation Launch I support you.
Now I have crossed and gone.
Gahonzire Mary, I am present
I will be spying from all corners
Nothing would come secretly to scare you
Nothing would disorganise you
I will apply my expertise
Education, nurturing and natural
At work, I am an expert
I will not be a dormant listener
Instead, I shall open my eyes and ears to the whole word
Rwanda will be respected and valuable to other countries
A Rwandan female shall be a role model.
In her home country and foreign land
Liberation Launch! I support you.
In his seat, Kayitare Emmanuel said,
I have heard it all. Liberation Launch! We are together
This is the time to tell you the secret
I discovered myself when I was young
I even told my parents
I was among those prophesied upon in my mother's womb
The day Rwanda will be in turmoil
There shall arise a warrior like Ruganzu
He will be a sacrifice to raise Rwanda from death to life
Its image shall surprise other countries
The foretellers confirmed that it was the time
I will be a sacrifice to liberate my people
On the day they will come across mad people dressed in rugs
Bathed in blood
The time will be closer

The Rwanda flowing into milk was protected by God
Now get up, it is time to go.
I have chosen to handle areas of Ruhengeri and Murera
I shall win and will have called a fierce Lion.
Liberation Launch I support you.
Nkusi Sam was there said
I will present to you the expertise I acquired from Europe.
Do not worry, I will establish radio Muhabura.
It will compete with those of our enemies
It will be confusion to them.
It will be sensitive to our people and they shall contribute
    surprisingly
These plans are unusual,
Let us just watch out
It shall not have a description; it will be called the Trinity
Liberation Launch I support it.
Rusagara Frank, I support the Liberation Launch.
I have been dreaming about Rwanda
Dreaming of fighting at the frontline.
And people were wondering and say
This young boy has championed the liberation
He moved his steps like Nyiringango
Armed with the shield.
I also dreamed of overcoming our enemies
The enemies wondering who these warriors are
We are growing up!
Let us Liberate Rwanda.

Nziza Jack said, you will not leave me
We shall go together

Being a Mufumbira means a Munyarwanda
Our policies do not shame us
The borders were set by foreigners
I should not fear
Or become a coward
Liberation Launch I support it.
Kayonga Charles, it is right we should go
Let me first go on top of hills in Kigali
I will be monitoring them without knowledge
Because of the expertise I shall have
They will suspect me according to the number I will give
    them
I will not fear complicated areas
I will spy and prepare a proper route
With patience and sacrifice
We shall lead our people to their homeland.
Liberation Launch I support it.
Mbandahe Mbayire Alfonse received the news
We in Rwanda in secret way
This Launch was all along awaited
Many years have passed when we are called cockroach
Come on and we will leave these gluttons
We shall be given deserving victorious names
We shall lead you in proper routes
Those in swamps and bushes

We shall crash the enemies and overcome them
Liberation Launch we support it.
The little boys, we have heard
You will not leave us behind even if you hider us

We shall follow you without your knowledge
When you will see us it will be too late
You cannot stop us, and then let us go to battle.
We will disguise ourselves among other children
And we shall have a great purpose,
To your surprise we will become heroes.
Liberation Launch we support it.
Students left their pens on desks
Those in Northern Uganda turned back and withdrew
Doctors left their overcoats in treatment rooms
Teachers gave themselves holidays
Some women were discharged
Children agreed that whether you like it or not
The time is up, they told their parents
Whether rain or shine we have gone
Don't be surprised, the time is now.
Get together; pray for us, we have gone to battle
So that we can take you back home.

Warriors or rebels liberated Rwanda in 1990, the group
crossed the border on 1-10-1990. Many of them came
from different countries from the entire world, they
provided different expertise. Those who returned from
their refugee have also joined, they are those who
sacrificed their lives, they are girls and boys, and we shall
always keep them in our hearts.

Boys and girls, I did not mention all names, but the few
names mentioned stand for others who have not been
mentioned.

Our warriors will never be forgotten because they are the

source of present Rwanda. We should not forget their parents, relatives and friends who supported them by contributing financially, their time, and providing various items which included among others; food, animals, when the last was physically got arms support the liberation struggle.

All these people should be recognised and thanked. This keeps us walking with our heads high and proud to be a Rwandans.

HUMURA SINAGUTANZE

Umwera atungutse iwacu yasanze ishyaka literwa nubumwe, asanga abantu alimbaga yinyabutatu atahamburwa nibihita, asanga basengera hamwe bagashyingirana bagahana igihango ngo badode ubwobumwe, bagatabalira hamwe Urwanda rukaba Rutinwya, bizwi ko rudaterwa ahubwo rutabazwa.

Umwera asanga ubwo bumwe buzabangamira

ubuhashyi bwamuhagurukije, ati: aliko nitwaje ikaramu nifaranga ndetse nimbunda na Bibilia.

Aduha itegeko ryokumuphukamira tugasengera mumateka yemereramo, ati: ndetse ntimugashyingirane muhujwe nubwo bumwe bwanyu, ahubwo mujje mushyingirana aruko muhuliye mumadini yacu.

Icyo nicyo cyingenzi cyahuzaga imiryango, ubwo amacakubiri atangira kuduseseramo atryo, ati ahubwo ndanababara mbihere ubwoko uko mbishyaka, ariko ndengere icyampagurukije.
Intwari Bisangwa wa Rugombituli azira iryo shyaka, azira ubwo bumwe, kuko basanze batazashobora

kumukoresha kucengezamo abahutu benewabo amacakubili.

Rukara rwa Bishingwe azira iryo shyaka azira ubwo bumwe kuko yanze agasuzuguro ko gutekererezwa.

Umwami Musinga acirwa ishyanga kuko yanze gutanga Urwanda kubwende, ati kirazira

Bakoresha ijambo ubwoko natwe turemera, twibagirwa umurage wabakurambere badusigiye, twibagirwa nurugero batweretse rulimo nurwa Rwabugili mubagore yarafite halimo umutwakazi bitaga Nturo yali yarubakiye kuku Busanza ka Runda

1959 Mutara aciye ubuhake niho ibintu mu Rwanda byatangiye gucika.

Rukabu amaze kubizira inkongi ikwira Urwanda
Ibitambambuga bijugunwa mumiliro ngo nibajje kuzimya ingo zabo.
Kuba Umuhutu bihabwa intebe, kuba Umututsi bitera isoni
Amazuru abura ahahishywa, igice kimwe cyabanyarwanda cyamburwa ubuntu girtyo.

Bati bariya ninzoka sabantu
Ndetse bamwe mubabuze aho bahisha amazuru bakwira amahanga, hashize kabili bati ni Nyenzi baragahera ishyanga. Imbuto Ntutsi abali Murwagasabo nabali hanze babura amahoro, aliko bati bucyana ayandi.

Abali mu Rwanda kubona ishuli nimilimo ukagura

Ubuhutu, cyanga hagahagararwa nabakobwa kubera ubwiza bahawe n'Imana, nuburere bahawe nababyeyi.

Igihe kiragera, hasohoka itegeko bati umutoni wa Leta kibe umuziro kurongora abatutsikazi, kuko sabo kwilingira, sabo kwiyegereza nimbuto ntindi.

Ahubwo tugiye kuvugurura imigambi yacu, tubatsembe burundu, abazavuka nyuma bazabaze icyumututsi yalicyo, bitali byabindi byaphubye kenchi ntibiduhire.

Kinani yongeye kurahira ngo abagiye bahere ishyanga.
Ati Urwanda nirutoya ntimwahakirwa, ninkikirahure cyuzuye amazi.
Abana bati reka reka Kinani ducyure ababyeyi, kuko kuneza kunabi turaza.

Kinani ati numureke baze byibura imigambi yarateguwe.
Bazaze baramutswe nibiti namabuye ababo twabatsembye.
Imambo zaratumiwe, imihoro iraza izabacagagura, amahili udufuni nudushoka birategurwa. Imyobo kabuhaliwe nimisarane ntibyibagiranye, bati nuwo tutazica azapha ahagaze, tuzamusige azaphe yumva azaphe nabi tukimureba.

Imilimo yarateguwe igihe kiragera
Barambara batangira ibyo bitaga akazi.
Uwo bahuye nawe bakareba ishusho.
Bati nturengaha ufite izuru nimisaya uruwogupha
Bati ntiwilirwe utakamba yamana yanyu yabatanze

Inzirakarengane baranze bakomeza kwizera iyo Mana basebeje.

Barebye amashusho bica nababo
Ukuyeho ko nabyo byali muligahunda
Byarateganirijwe italiki yabyo
Kuwaliwe wese wanduye amaraso ya Gatutsi
Aruwo kuzapha.

Bishe abantu muburyo bwinchi butavugika.
Bishe ababigenewe nabahutu bindahemuka barugenderamo.
Bashinze imambo mubali
Bazilika ababyeyi kubiti babakorera ibyamfurambi
Abakobwa beza bamatako meza ateye imbabazi barababaza
Abandi barabamba ngo niko Yezu yategetse.

Abishe bavuye munzego zose ningano zose.
Abasore ninkumi, abasaza nabacyecuru
Ndetse nibitambambuga byatese bitema.

Byagoye abagenewe gupha
Bayoberwa uwo bahungiraho
Bagumya kwizera yamana yabo basebeje.

Basatuye amada yababyeyi
ngo barebe uko abana babatutsi baryamye.
Mumatryazo ya Butare umugore Tamasha yaciye abandi
    bagore amabere
Ayo aramabere yonkeje imfura.
Aliko izonzira karengane bakomeye kuliyo Mana yasebejwe

Bajugunya abantu mubyobo kabuhaliwe alibazima.
Ibitambambuga bati nimube muretse turatokorwa.
Abandi bati nimutureka none ntituzongera kuba abatutsi
Bati Imana yanyu yabatanze nimuphe.

Bajugunwe mumisarane nomumigezi
ahatembaga amazi hatemba amaraso
Muzabaze Muhazi na Nyabarongo
Muzabaze Victolia aho amasamake yahagaritswe kurobwa
Muzabaze abagande baroba abana
batunze kubiti nka mushikake.
Aho mumazi banyuzwaga ngo niyubusamo.

Abadafite amafaranga yokugura isasu ryokubarasa
Bagacocagurwa
Babasaba kubica ngo baveho bati aliko ibyanyu byose
     mushaka ibyiza?
nogupha nabyo ra! Noneho nimuphe nabi.

Baratemaguwe baracocagurwa
Ndetse udatatse ngo atakambe bakabimwibutsa.
Abagore bishe abana babo bonkeje
kuko bibutse ko bababyaye kumbuto mbi
Abandi bica abishwa cyanga abobashakanye.

Abahandi bati amashitani yisi yose yimukiye mu Rwanda.

Basanga icyabatabara aruguhungira mubilizia,
Bilingiye Leta yi Iroma kuko arabayoboke
Bati abamakanzu nibitambaro baragira impuhwe.

Aliko barahageze bati murakaza mboga zizanye.

Ibiliziya babibalimbuliraho ngo kubatsemba biborohere
Ibindi bahamagalizwa inkora maraso bati baragwiliye.
Dore ko bali bateguye kubashyirahamwe
Kuko ngo nutwika imbagara abanza akazejjeranya
Inzirakarengane ntibatezutse kuli yamana basebeje.

Naje guhura naya Mana nkubita amavi hasi ndayibaza
Ntese Mana muremyi nkubaze,nikoko burya abange
    warabatanze?
Imana mijwi linini cyane lihindira
Ryahinze kwisi hose igahungabana
Yarambwiye iti humura mwana wange sinabatanze.
Iyo mbatanga ntanumwe uba warasanze.

Iti inkoramaraso baribeshye barababeshya
Sinabatanze sinabatanga kwikora munda.
Iti burya nijje washyize umujinya wubutwali Muzamarere
Bakizilika imyenda munda nkababyaye
Ngobayihekeshe imbabare zange aho bazisanze

Uwabo umwe warabibonye ngo arashorera abangomeye
    ibihumbi.
Ubwo imyotsi yabacumbaga kumitwe bayitekeyeho umugenda.

Izamarere batanguranwa nasakabaka nimbwa bibalira ababo.
Babatora ahobali, bahumeka badahumeka
Babatera imugongo babasubiza ibumuntu.
Warabibonye babahashya Ikibeho

aho bali bubikiliye ngobagaruke ntibanyuzwe
Nibidaterurwa bya Abafaranca kuko batashize uko bashaka.
Izamarere nijje wabashyizemo ubwo bwema mwana wange.

Burya igihe cyange cyali cyigeze
cyokwiyegereza abange intore zange.
Kandi mbasigiye inchungu nahaye ubutwali numurava.
Naho imbuto Ntutsi nayihanze kubwende, kandi nyihanga
    nyikunze.
Abiyemeje kunkora mujisho nabavumye nk, Imana
Ngo bazaphe umugenda banyure kuli Goma bagere
    Tingitingi.
Kandi iteka aho bazaba bari hose ijisho ryange ryigishilira
    bajje baryikanga

Aliko icyombabujije nuguhora
Ibyo nibyange birandeba
Numushyigikire ubumwe nabaraze gakondo
Muzababarire ariko ntimuzibagirwe
Ahubwo reka nkugire intumwa yange, uzabitangalize abandi
Ko ubu nahinduye gahunda.

Sinkilirwa ahandi ngo ntahe i Rwanda bwije.
Urwagasabo nahagize IJABIRO ryange.
Niho mba amasaha makumyabili nane, ahandi hirya hino
    hose kwisi
Nkahalindisha UBUKAKA BWANGE

Humura Rwanda humura bana bange sinabatanze.

DON'T BE FEARFUL,
I DIDN'T GIVE
UP TO YOU

Once colonials emerge in our motherland he discovers the
unity of toughness among people
Society of trinity who are never divided by anything and
worship together

We exchange intermarriage among us, we exchange life reliance
among us in order to build on that rock-solid unity
He recognises we hold up each other and protect and attack
as one Rwanda is treasured
Rwanda attacks not attacked; instead Rwanda interferes
where it requires peace

The imposing discover the unity will contest their own
interest to convey him here

He says: I'm confident. I come with pens, money, with guns
plus bibles as well
He ordered us to our knees for him play and believes in his
own faith

Furthermore he opposed us to marry each other to break the
value of our unity

That was most important to unity, family-division started to
be inserted in our culture

He started to count us and created ethnics like he wanted to
divide us in order to guard his interest

He counted wealth and gave us ethnic as he planned, he
inherited the curse

Hero Bisangwa WA Rugombituli, paid a big price of his life
for his courage and unity and his country

The colonials realise they won't able to use him to mobilise
his Hutu ethnic hatred division

Rukara rwa Bishingwe pay a big price of his life because he
refuses the arrogance and slavery.

King Musinga became their No 1 enemy because he refused
just to give up Rwanda easily; he says it is a curse in
Rwandan tradition to surrender Rwanda. Instead you
give your life defending Rwanda

They used ethnicity and we agreed, we forget our inheritance
of our ancestors

We forget our good examples of our predecessor including
King Rwabugiri.

Who has had Twa ethnic named Nturo as one of his wives?

In 1959 King Mutara abolished slavery in Rwanda and things
started to look bad

Rukabu, after paying price, the flame of fire spread through
all Rwanda

The toddlers' thoroughness out in the fire intentionally

saying they use them to take out fire of their own parents

Being Hutu become superior and being Tutsi become a disgrace

There is no way you can hide your nose, one party of Rwandan people stripped their own humanity.

They says Tutsi are snakes, they're not human

Some fled Rwanda into overseas countries and they changed language Instead of being snakes they said they're cockroaches and we don't want them back in Rwanda forever.

Tutsi inside the country were harassed, discriminated against, even killed slowly

Tutsi in foreign countries were able to integrate and they changed their own name to get a school and win with higher marks.

The ones who stayed in Rwanda to find a school and work become tough, some they have to buy Hutu ethnicity.

The time arrive the policy declare no Hutu in administration or military allowed to get married to the Tutsi women because we can't trust them, we don't want them amongst us, they're horrific people.

Instead we desire to chase them out of our country and wipe them until our new generation will ask in future what Tutsi looked like

Kinani, former Rwanda President insist Rwanda is too small, there is no place for Tutsi, it is like glass full of water if you add one drop of water some water will be squandered

Rwandan in outside asked for dialogue saying Rwanda is our home too and is where our heart is, we want to come back with our parents in peaceful way or fighting for our right.

Kinani, former Rwanda President says ok let them come, our plan is ready, they will welcomed with sticks and stones after the massacre of their own relatives in this country, the machetes are ready delivered, guns, grenades, etc...

They set up the training camp to train how to kill Tutsi as job training, as they say when they finish the killing, we finish our job

They mobilised to butcher the Tutsi and Hutu moderates, who opposed slaughter and would not help to kill

They say we're ready, waiting to pull a trigger and start to chop them, rape the women, burn them alive, wipe them off face of the earth

Time comes, get ready and start work, and they set up road blocks all over the country checking identity. Even physical appearance can get you killed, they say. Don't even beg for mercy, even your god deserted you but the victims resist to lost faith in god.

By checking physical appearance they killed even their own ethnicity, even if it was planned to kill everybody who has mixed blood with Tutsi after wiping out all pure Tutsis.

They killed Tutsi in many ways you can never imagine,

They killed Tutsis, even moderate Hutu who try to hide Tutsi

They raped the women, young or old, even grandmothers

The beautiful young girls raped and some have been crucified on the cross

The killers come from all ages, genders and all areas

Young men and girls, old men and women, even teenagers

It was very hard for Tutsi, there was no way for refuge, and they had been hunted like animals

They had been ambushed all over; they were just waiting to die wherever you go

They have no where to go, everwhere killing was on,
    everwhere it was devil work
But they never lost hope and belief in god.
They cut the pregnant women to see what a Tutsi foetus
    looks like
In Matyazo of Butare District one woman was called
    TAMASHA, reaper of other women's breasts
The breast who fed another human being, good people
They threw people in big holes which were made for that
    reason, toilets and lakes when they were still alive!
The area of flood water became flood of blood
Muhazi and Nyabarongo rivers turned into baths of blood
Fish from Victoria Lake stopped being eaten
The fishermen from Uganda, instead of catching fish, they
    caught toddlers' bodies in the lake
They threw them in the lake as a shortcut to return them
    where they say they come from

The person who doesn't have money to buy bullets to be
    used to kill him
They have been butchered like dead meat
They've begged to be killed with bullets and the response
    was no because always Tutsi want the best
Even deaths! No you have to suffer even in dying
They've been hacked to death, even make them suffer much
The women killed their own children saying having them
    with Tutsi is a curse
Others killed their own wifes, relatives; just simply because
    they're mixed with Tutsi blood
People think Rwanda is full of demons

They think shelter in churches is the only way away from
    demons
Hoping fathers and sisters are full of grace
Instead they welcome them with no help and called the killer
    to kill them

They destroyed churches on top of them
They even organised to put them together
Because they say if you want to burn wood you put them
    together
The victims never lost the faith in god

I meet god and fall on my knee and ask
My god creator of everything, is it true you have given up my
    people
God reply to me in loudest sound and powerfully to shake
    the world
He says: No don't be fearful my child, I don't give up on you
If I had given up on you no one would have survived
God says, I didn't give up on you, I didn't give up on you
How could I give up on my own people?
I'm the one who gives courage and heroism in RPF Inkotanyi
Using everything possible to save the victims and defeat the
    demons
FPR Inkotanyi did everything in a short time to save as many
    as they can save
They pick up the casualities, still breathing or not, put them
    on the shoulder
You saw how they defeated them in Kibeho when the killer
    had strong weapons from the French

You saw how only one of them defeated thousands of them?
   That was me who was giving them all of that braveness.
Don't be frightened, I didn't give up my people.

All who have been killed are with me in my house
They're in my glory where it is reserved for them.

Those who killed them, I cursed them and I'll watch them
   wherever they are

I warned you don't try for revenge
That it is my work only to judge and punish them
Promote, unite and restore your unity I have inherited a long
   time ago
Forgive, don't forget, that message I give you to tell Rwanda

I don't stay away and return in Rwanda in the evening any
   more
Instead Rwanda rwa Gasabo is now my blessed home
Don't be troubled, I didn't give up on my people.

EQUALITY

Ooo I want the whole world to know and have an equality.
Equality of imagination.
I am fighting for my right
I want it to be known that I am alive
I want to be recognised by society
Without equality people show power and become greedy.
Create conflict, homelessness and death.
Then refugees and asylum seekers.
Look at Sudan, Iraq, Afghanistan, Syria, Libya…
So
Please let us have equality.
And what equality?
Equality is confidence
Is hope and life.
Be happy to see others equal, by that you are giving them
    confidence, hope and life.
Where they are equals you can't see any kind of slavery,
    racism or bullying.
Don't give away what you have, if you don't want to, but give
    them equality.
With it we can save ourselves some gap between rich and
    poor, we see children kill themselves because of bullying.
Why can someone shoot 170 bullets in only nine minutes to
    kill?

Many times because they hate themselves and hate others too!

They bereave that they don't have equality and they lose confidence.

They bereave that other people caused them misery

Cho Seung –Hui, a young man of 23 years old, showed this in April 2007 in America when he killed 33 people before he killed himself.

Let us try to live with others in an equal way.

So that we can save ourselves some misery in our lives.

I want to see equality in the whole world.

FAREWELL TO THE KING

At five years old he was the King
He changed his appearance
But hadn't changed his heart.

He was not white
And he was not black
He was the world.

He didn't want the world to turn him
Around from his dream,
Indeed he changed the world
With his magic of dancing
Moon walking and creation
Of neutral sound.

He changed the world
With his genius
Gentleness and generosity
And made him reach his dream
To become the world.
He was a fighter who never stops
Until he was up where he wanted to be.

He knows that in life there are times
You have to keep on trying and no
Matter what be unchangeable
And fight for your personality.

With his sweetest and humanitarian heart
It was easy for him to reach his dream
To become the world.

He managed to give many hope
Confidence, happiness and smile
He taught them how to love and how to live.

He took them from a dark period
And made them be better in their lives.
He gives them treasure
In their heart he was huge
Part in their lives.
He was and he will be their
Hero for ever and ever.

He was a giant King who wanted
To heal the world and the people
Through his music, art, love, decency?
He has knowledge he has succeeded.
He was their shining light.
He showed them that
If you believe you can.
He was the most recognised
Most well know and the most

Loved person on our planet for 45 years.

No one can ever possibly be him.
He is in the Guinness book
Of world records for his music
And for helping others.
In the 1980s he helped Ethiopia
From hunger with the song *We Are The World*.
He was the gift to the world.
He was simply the greatest entertainer that ever lived.
He was a money making machine.
To hell with child abuse, they wanted his money

Michael Jackson: he was the king of music at his time.

And he loved by young and old.

FAREWELL TO THE KING
NO. 2

He doesn't accept limitations.
He refused to let people decide his boundaries.
He broke down the colour curtains.
He didn't let himself sink, always
Managed to swim no matter what.

His child like ways to others.
People wanted a piece of him
Wanted to touch him, to feel him.
To feel him and to love him.
Many wanted to be like him
And to be with him.

He had driven to the top himself and
He had Neverland ranch...
He was the best ever we could imagine.

Some loved him more than themselves
Rightly his life has a lot more add twists
In the road than many
Michael was like part of their soul.
They can't help it that is the way it was.

Death is damned death.
On 25 June 2009 the King of Pop was dead.
It was big shock around the world
Whatever race, colour, creed or culture

It was so soon, he went in a sudden way
And his death was big, tragic and a mystery.

It broke their hearts, people were
Disappointed with his death
Especially when they heard rumours
Of murder involved.
Some, they killed themselves
Others won all who loved the King.
That Michael wouldn't be happy with that
That he loved people and wanted them
To be happy in his life time and in his death time.

If they have to cry
They have to cry
But through it all try to rise above it.
And be strong to their pop icon.

It was hard to believe
It was so unreal that Michael had gone
It was deep and emotional. As bizarre in death as he was in life.
His originality changed the
Land of music forever.
One of the most widely global
Beloved entertainers

And profoundly influential artists
Of all time on popular music
And culture has gone.
But we will remember forever and ever.

Can you feel it?
Can you tell the happiness he gives the people?
Can you feel the love he loved them?
Can you tell how they loved him back?
Can you feel the disappointment and
Pain his friends, family and all who loved him have?

He was not a strange man
But he had to deal with strange things.
That most famous man, notorious star
On the planet, he was the father, son,
Brother, uncle, friend, but more than
That he was the world.

His death was one of the most
Astonishing days witnessed in America.
People wanted him back
He was too young to die.
Michael born rich and died rich

Too many had tattoos
Of his name on their body.
Felt that part of him will be with them
Forever and part of them went with him.

They had to be strong for Michael's
Legacy and remember that he taught them
To be the best of what they are and strong
To whatever comes in front of you.
That is Michael Jackson.

GOODBYE TO
KING OF POP

The farewell of the King
Was the greatest show on earth.

Greeted by a gospel choir
Singing Hallelujah.
We are going to see the King.

His farewell was bigger
Than Elvis's and Princess Diana's.
Once Michael Jackson said
That his own funeral was likely
To be the greatest show on Earth.

And that is how it was.
It was watched by millions
Of people around the world.
There were big numbers
Of police officers
Private security teams
Patrolled the event.

Elephants, Tigers, Zebras

And ponies from Ringling
Bros and Barnum
Bailey circus passed
Through downtown L A.

Dozens of LAPD motorcycle
Outriders and the city's
SWAT teams
Cars like Range Rovers
Rolls Royces, Cadillacs, buses
ambulances, police helicopters
Several squad cars...
It was the largest security
Operation LA has ever seen.
Just because of the King

They were all kinds of people
With big names
Actors, politicians
Civil rights campaigners.
It reminded the world
The legacy of the showbiz
He has left behind.

People in every corner of the world
Whatever their race
Colour or creed, they were lost for words.
Michael was very meek
Was great in his death
As when he was in life.

They warn that up to a million
Could show up
But organisers managed
To limit the numbers.

Some were selling their personal
Possessions to pay for the trip.
Front of them they were not seeing
Discovered with red roses.

But they see his golden heart
His genuine way of life
His childlike and his
Innocent way of life to them.

People came from all across casino
The moment which will forever go
Down in the history the world to witness
The spectacular accession
The moment which will forever go
Down in history not only in America
But all over the world.

One global respected person at time
Nelson Mandela, S Africa
Among others in his message say
That Michael was a giant and a legend
In the music industry
And he mourn with millions
Of fans worldwide the loss of their dear friend.

Yes, the giant has gone but will live forever.
And the world can't forget Michael Jackson
He will be here ever and ever
Born August 29, 1958, died June 25, 2009.

FORGIVE

There are sins you can forgive or
Pretend to forgive, but can't forget
My Africa, full of love
Peace and unity, of immeasurable richness.
Your history is here to stay. 1434
The first Europeans set foot in Africa
Things started to change
Not for better but for death.
They robbed ten or twenty million African children
Passed through a lot
Of different trials and tribulations.
Tied up like a goat,
Thrown in the water alive, beaten, and raped!
They loved Africa and made love to Africans
At the same time
Enjoyed seeing Africans die in slow motion.
They robbed them of their culture, their identity,
Their dignity.
They gave Africa a new map,
No African leader was present!
And they called it international law!
Africa, mixed up with culture, languages,
Inter-marriages and confusion.

Africans dying from anger and hunger.
Poverty was the leader.
War after unnecessary wars
African children dying day and night.
"Look," you can hear them say, *"look how Africans are killing each
    other, how they are greedy."* These dictators. This corruption
The children don't go to school
Don't have shoes and still they are dying from hunger.
Brave Africa
Yet Africa doesn't have to be tied up
With the past, follow your examples.
Wake up, wake up Africa
Follow the example of Mandela and forgive,
But don't forget.
A time will come when you say
Enough is enough.
Rwandans refuse to be tied up to the past,
They have to forgive,
To forgive each other, and look to the future,
But not to forget.
Children of Africa in Europe and America,
You have suffered in the name of slavery,
But don't be tied up with the past,
Forgive or pretend forgive, but don't forget,
Look to the future.
Together build back the continent,
My Africa, full of love
Forgive.

THE FUTURE CAPITAL OF PALESTINE

Every man's wish is freedom
And Obama's is echoed in the change we need
To fight against violent extremism
Reject radical ideologies
Respect human kind
And more and more than anything
A belief in the legitimacy of the two states
Israel and Palestine

I share this belief.
As
Both states share an intertwined history.

It is not Jerusalem that is the problem
It is the mind of the people
To realise that
Unity is the key

Can you feel it? My tears are dried but my heart is bleeding.

Are we so uncaring
That we let our young ones fight

Bullets and with stones
Our young men, women and men
Die in a cause I believe can be averted

It is not Jerusalem
It is us
We have stopped caring about ourselves
Life has become meaningless

We have become militant
And we have people we classify as infidels
No one is a brother!

I don't hate Palestine and I don't hate the Jewish. What I want
    is equality

If we have to share let us share

Let the oasis of love flow
Let the trumpet of hate stop
Let anger dissipate
And just watch
How the blood will stop to flow
For it stop!!
Let the future capital of Palestine
Be in the heart!

Let us fight with map maker when and where is necessary
If it can help to serve life
Time is now to say that enough is enough.

Give women a chance to be happy, to have babies, and give
   hope to a future generation: hope of life.
Let the Holy City of Jerusalem be an example of peace, not
   an example of death.

By Kwesigwa Sammy Muvunangoma

HARD TIME

No one who can want hard time to knock the door.
They are time when can be hard time.
No one ever wish to come across those times
Sometimes you can be alone and lonely.
That is hard time.
Even when you have a lot at that time you can't see.
The eyes can see them but not the heart.
At that you wish to know where to buy peace of your heart.
You wish to give your soul enough protection
To be away from loneliness and give it love
Even if it can ask you to give away your wealth.
You didn't want to hate yourself just because you had a hard
    time.
But sometimes you can do that, which is hard time.
That is when someone thinks about taking away her/his life.
Believe that no need to be alive.
That is when you wish you can get somewhere to buy peace.
Where to buy love.
And to go away from loneliness.
And maybe hatred.
All you see is hard time.
When the health become upside down.
Your health or your loved ones.

At that time no matter how much you have.

Your eyes will see it but not your heart.

What you have will not matter anymore.

You will want to get where you can buy good health.

So that you can feel better.

So that you can feel normal.

You can do whatever you can, to see that you get back your
health.

You want to help the loved one who the health

Is refusing to help her or him

But you don't know how.

After to do all you can

You wish to carry her or his suffering.

But you can't.

You wish to reduce or to finish his or her pain.

But you can't.

That is hard time.

Don't think about the last time when you lose the loved one.

That time is hard time.

Sometimes you don't want someone to say sorry.

They understand how you feel.

Because you can't believe that person.

How you feel is deep down far in you.

Deep in your soul

No one can see and understand how.

When you know that no one who can repress the loved one.

That is hard time.

Time can pass

Memories can fade

Feelings can change.

People can leave.
But hearts never forget.
Pray that hard time can't ever knock at your door.

HOPE

I have a hope that one day everyone is going to be equal. Equal, not because of money, not because of his or her originality, but only because of all of us we are human beings. I have a hope that one day people are going to be happy to stay alive everywhere they will be.

I have a hope that one day Africa is going to be one.

I have a hope that African people will see how badly hate between them, greed and to be used, is damaging their future and future generation, when some still use excuses of history.

Hope that time will come, to go back to their original culture of love and unity.

And see how love and unity is strong weapon and is everything in life.

African people, these days they travel around the world. They see different culture and characters. I have a hope that this is going to help them to come back to their original culture, culture of love and unity which will help them to make Africa one.

I am old lady who was born and grown up in Africa all of my life until 2004 when I come out of my continent for the first time.

I didn't know the beauty of Africa and African people until I was out and away from that beauty. That is how and when I come to get a good picture of why African people were tortured for so long time, since slavery time until now there are still a problem of free market... but I have a hope.

In all of that time they were given the disease of killing their culture, culture of love and unity, which was a long illness and slow deaths.

No matter that Africa is rich with good resources, 80 per cent or more of African people have stayed very poor while the rest stay very rich. But I have a hope.

In my life, being people who like to mix with different people, I thought that I knew European people and their life, but when I lived in Britain in November 2004, I realised that I know nothing about them.

At first I was able to talk to some people, but others was a problem because of my accent.

It took me time to be used to their culture. I used to say hello on the street back home, but here when I say hello to someone, sometimes they look at me as if I am crazy, instead go back to talk to their dogs! Don't expect that your neighbour will knock on your door to say good morning, and don't do that to them either, because they might call the police if you knock on their doors.

But not all of them. There are a small number of people who were happy to help and if I asked to go somewhere they were ready to show me or to take me there.

I read somewhere in one of the newspapers in 2004, that in Germany, they want to start a school to teach people to laugh because they'd forgotten about it. Then I thought that even in Britain they need a school like that, because a big number of people have the same problem. There are some who are left only with what they call a smile; this is to pull their lips to the sides for half a second.

I come to meet a lot of old people who told me that they have never had a family for themselves and it was their choice, but instead they stay with their pets. So, to me, seems that is why they look as if they don't have enough contact with people and the good friends they have are their animals.

Maybe that is why some leave their fortune to the animals when they die.

Others have separated from their families for many years and they have forgotten each other. Someone told me that if he met his children he wouldn't recognise them when they still living in the same area! There is a lady, my friend, who told me that she doesn't know if her mum is still alive or died! She doesn't know anything about her for over twenty years!

And when you talk to a person like that for some time, no matter how much money he/she has, they do not have a happy life.

I come to see some cases in the news, of children, sometimes fifteen years old and below, where they go together in big numbers and enjoy killing old people or other children! They even advise parents to carry their babies on their front side to keep them safe; when back home they know that back side is best side and comfortable for their babies.

That is a kind of life which I never saw in Africa. I felt sorry and it hurts me to see some young African people, who came in West countries knows that they came to heaven, ending up cut communication with their families back home because of the bad situation they are in. But I have a hope.

I have a hope that in future the majority of African children are going to be happy and proud to stay in their countries and to gather to build their continent.

And don't think that if you get a British passport you are

recognised as full British. They are very careful here, because you have to remember to remind them who you are, every time you want something, when you fill some forms at that time you have to show your ethnic origin.

But on the other hand, this is good; some can be comfortable and forget that they come from somewhere else.

Before in Africa it was taboo and a curse to kill someone except in war, yes I came to see why in Britain they try everything to encourage people to be good to their neighbours by giving medals to someone who was good to others. Something which, to Africans, even their culture had seeds of hatred for long time, they still have in them, that their neighbours are like a member of their family, so it is their responsibility to help each other, at least 90 per cent. And the rest, history is judging them. But I have a hope.

After 1994, when genocide happened in my country Rwanda, genocide which happened in front of the whole world and everyone was watching as if it was a film.

Rwandan people started reconciliation which was a very hard step but they had to do it, and it was successful day by day.

I have a hope.

I AM WHO I AM

I am who I always wanted to be
I am me.
Changes didn't manage to change me
Hunger and anger didn't change me
I am who I always wanted to be
I am me.
I am mother and grandmother
I give peace and I give love, I mediate.
I am fighter and I am survival.
Ancient histories of pain didn't change me. I am who I am
I am who I always wanted to be
I am me.
They are time I was behind
They are time I was in motion
They are time I was vigorous
They are time I was exhausted
And they are time I was in danger
But nothing changed me
I am who I always wanted to be
I am me
Limitation of education didn't tied me back.
I am who I always wanted to be.
People wonder where my secret lies

Most of them see it as a mystery.
Something which makes me proud
Nothing managed to change me.
Racism didn't change me
I use my magic to be leader and ladder
I am honest with myself. I am who I am
I am who I always wanted to be
Black beauty, a writer, I am the universe
I am who I always wanted to be.
I am me.

I HAD A MOTHER

Mother
Who was too beautiful
Medium height
Medium weight
Beautiful smile
With shining black beauty
But people loved her for her good heart.
Kindness with good advice
Helping everyone around her.
That mother we both knew.
We have her photo in our heads and hearts
Whose countenance moulded the contours of our own, in
Those marrows pulsed primordial blood
From a deep well of knowing
Her glances met ours, seeking
In close comfort we were carried
On her supple back
On her powerful hip
There was permission
To shelter in the landscape of her back, her breast
To stroke her soft black hair with wonder
To take refreshment from the clear pools of her eyes
Whose clear gaze gave back her own constancy.

We, children and mother born to this mechanical peace
Where glances are badly timed.
And her joy was that we blood bond of an unbroken bond
Should survive her and in courage, bring others whose
Clear gaze back her own constancy
Take one, add two, add three and four, then five and six
We, children born
To this mechanical age where glances are badly timed
Joy was that of we blood of her blood
(Daughter to mother, mother to daughter) both daughters
    and sons
Both sense the measure of loss
Yet pound to her great body
In flight from dangers on camel's back
On moccasin trails
In dreams we are not altogether bereft.
Mother to daughter, daughter to mother.
Our beautiful mother.
Bagorebeza
We will be with us always in our hearts.

JOURNEY

Always journey, which always hard
Journey is hard for us
This journey has no mercy to anyone
Except those who are lucky.
Let me call this journey
Journey of struggle
This journey has no respect, no fear of us.
It does not mind if you are a scholar,
Rich, young, wise, beautiful, just hold your breath.
It will take you up and down.
Many times to reach the end of it, you need to be still.
Hoping and waiting, what tomorrow brings.
Say tomorrow and wait for tomorrow
Sometimes the more you try,
The more you are disappointed
Then you ask yourself.
Why me? Why me?
The journey seems cruel
Cruel and painful
Especially when the journey carries you faraway
Away from your people,
When you lose your loved one
When you think that no one cares about you

Some few people are lucky ones
So lucky because they
Have everything needed in the world
The four important things in life
Good health, happy family, love and money.
True enough, this journey.
Is the journey of life?
Journey of life means journey of struggle.

LUCK

What is luck?

Many of us we believe something called luck, luck in
   different ways.

Or luck in all ways.

Some ways of luck, we create them ourselves, or many, if
   not all.

You can count yourself to be the lucky one, depending
   what is in front of you.

Count yourself the lucky one, if your work or your family
   doesn't colonise neither dictate to you.

But why can't you see your luck, when you see day and
   night? See yourself lucky if your children they are not
   breathing in swilling dust and the noisy life.

When your children don't eat little and die young.

When your sister, daughter or mother didn't get raped by
   gangs.

When a loved one, someone close to you doesn't die or half
   die because of feeding herself/himself with drugs in
   her/his vein.

When no one close to you dies or half dies, because of
   ignorance.

Ignorance of power or family members, all because of
   selfishness.

Count yourself to be lucky, when do not dislike yourself
because of who you are.
Maybe because of your disability, or you can't do much like
so and so.
You are worried because you are too dark or too light.
Because you are unloved as a child.
You are not worried that they are talking behind your back.
You don't mind what others think about you, and you have
full confidence to do what you think is better.
Then count yourself to be lucky, especially when someone
tells you that she/he loves you.
The love which is not covered in any shining pursuits of
business.
And know that the power of love, doesn't have to turn to
be the love of power.
When you are not creating many different planets in one.
When you know that the best things in life aren't things.
When you can be able to love yourself, and have time to
think about your neighbour.
When you feel free to run the riot, and fight for your
survival, to have your freedom.
And most of that: when you're proud of your history.
Count yourself to be the lucky one.

CONGRATULATIONS BUT THIS, IT IS THE BEGINNING

I feel alive when I write
I want you to know why I write
But I fear to write it here
Because I am the victim of the truth

I refuse to keep quiet
I want you to read my poem
My poem is poem of pain
OOO no no no
My poem is not poem of pain
My poem is poem of celebration.

Let me say how it was
They treated you as a monster
When they turned themselves into monsters
With hate race, all of that simply because of your colour.
Your heritage
They put you in prison
Prison of fear
Fear of yourself
By bereave that you can't.

For those years of suffering
Years and years of teaching
Chant, chant, teach, teach and cheating

In verses but riches tortures
From your mothers crashed your lives
Forget this wound in the earth
Forget this scar in your hearts
Mark the grave your heart

You lived a life of neglect
What you wanted at that time
Was room of justice?
They clenched your mind
They killed you by ideologies
In such of directions
You refused to perish
You refused to die that day

You didn't die yesterday
You waited to be recognised

And now it is your beginning
To have your dignity
To love yourselves
To be free at last
Thank God our God
To be here today and see this celebration
And now you have your dreams
Let us sing Harerujaaaa

In the whole world with all races
Now no black, no white or Asian
We are the universe.

No more time of slavery
Time of dying again and again
Let me mark that grave of your soul
And be able to test happiness
Just keep your history
That once your color was shame
But now it is time to know that black is beauty.

Let me salute Oprah and others
Who was behind the struggle?
To help the mother to give birth to your dream
Martin Luther King's dream
That birth was not easy
That birth was long journey
That birth was hard struggle
They had a hope and behind the mother
Mother push, push, and puuuush

I am pushing
I am trying
But at last the child was born
The baby kicked his legs
Kicked that wall of his mind
The mind of change
Ahahaaaa
Was gasp of joy?

Your heart banging doors
Doors of dreams
Doors of freedom
I saw doors opening in slow motion
At last you have your beginning
You don't mind if they wanted him for their reasons
You have him for your dreams

It is you Michelle Obama
Congratulations Michelle
From slavery to first lady of United States of America
It is our honour Michelle

This it is the beginning
But at last you have the beginning.

Congratulations Mrs Obama

NAME

What is a name?
A name is an identity for everything
Say a name I will know what you mean
Animal, tree, water, food all have names
But different names
Planets too, have names.
Our planet which we have today has a name
We have different continents, with different countries
And different names.
We too, human beings we have names
Names which are our identity
When we say our names
It helps us to know where we come from
Which country, sometimes which area and which community.
Me too, I have a name.
Ooo my name!
Bamurangirwa is my name
I am proud to have my name.
My name is everything to me.
The meaning of my name, it shows me my parents' love for me
My beauty, my name represents my country and my
    community.
I thank very much my parents, Bagorebeza and Sinzi

My parents, who gave me my name
I am proud of my name.
Bamurangirwa comes from (kuranga) announce.
You announce something you are sure of
Something you believe in
And something you are proud of that it will not let you down.
I am happy I didn't let them down
Name is identity.

QUESTION

I have a question

A question about foreigner religions in foreign countries.

Don't get me wrong, I believe in God. I respect people with their beliefs.

But I give more respect to those who still stand to their original religions.

Some people say that God is a man, because a man is strong and better to govern.

Others say that God is a woman because a woman is kind and very careful.

There are those who say that God is white because white people are clever

But some say that God is black, because black people are original of human beings.

I don't ask who God is, I believe that God is God, and God is one.

If so, why foreigner religions in foreigner countries?

Soon after to be in foreigner countries with their religions, they have competitions as if they have many different Gods they are working for?

And when that countries, they believe in God, and pray in their ways, but the foreigner religions will tell them that their way is not the right way to pray.

One will say that my way is only the right way to reach to God spiritually and also to be with God after death.

Others will come and say the same thing. That his/her religion is better!

They will try to brain wash you to show you that to reach your God spiritually you have to follow their history, and tell you that they know God better according to their history not yours.

In that work of God some they argue or fight!

Some people just follow without knowing what is going on, just because they see others there.

And there are those who follow when they feel that is the way to help them to reach their God.

There are others who go there because they are depressed or to show off.

But leaders, some of them the big reason is political and a way of becoming rich quickly.

Why these foreign religions in foreign countries?

I still have question.

SOMETIMES

Sometimes you get bad news.
And you don't know why.
And you ask yourself over and over
And sometimes say why you?

But this is happening to us.
In different ways, sometimes.
From people we loved and trusted.

And believed that they loved us and trusted us.
But sometimes we can be disappointed.
When we need to be loved and trusted.
Those times you ask yourself why?
And many times you ask yourself why you?

When you knew that you tried to put fire on.
Because love is fire
If you don't put it on, it will go off.
But you have done your part.
Still you were disappointed, you will ask yourself why.
And ask yourself why you?
But you have to carry on and on, and have life.

Sometimes we get bad news
And we don't know why.
From family or friends.
You can trust a friend and do what you can do.
To make a friend happy.
Little do you know that a friend is going behind your back.
Then you become disappointed.
And ask yourself why?
And sometimes ask yourself why you?

But you have to carry on and have life.

Sometimes
You plan things with a hope to be a success.
But instead it becomes a big problem to you.
And you ask yourself why?
And ask yourself why you?

Sometimes when you are lucky to be a success in life.
People around you will say that they knew.
That you had to be a success no matter what.
Because you are hard working, or you are clever.

But sometimes when your way is shut.
People around you will say that they knew.
That nothing you can be able to manage.
Because you are lazy, or this and that.
But you have to carry on with life.

Sometimes, but some other times, your day

Can be a lucky day, and luck knocks on your door.
No matter how hard and strong you locked the door.
The luck will enter your door anyway!
And you will not believe your eyes.
That it is you who have your dream.
That your dream comes to be true.
And you will never forget that day.

And
Sometimes.
Some other times.
Sometimes, things can change, and change.
And change in the right or the left.
Better you take it how it is.
And carry on with your life no matter what.

Don't let anything change you, just be you.

That is how you will be a winner.

That is only sometimes.

STRUGGLE

They had to struggle for survival, survival for themselves and
    their family, because they had to leave their country.
They were young and beautiful but they had to struggle.
They were loved by their parents but they faced hardship.
Every one of them had to strive in order to survive.
People endeavour in different ways
At times they can be successful in days.
At times it can make them stronger. Be more sympathetic,
    caring and live longer.
They were like solders in they own ways.
They promised themselves that they will fight for the
    wellbeing of their families
Do wherever will come in front of them.
In those years. Years and years.
Years of suffering, years of growing up.
Years of trying, trying and trying.
Years of love, the loved ones, and do wherever it takes to see
    them happy.
To see them alive.
They wanted their young brothers and sisters to have a
    future.
A proper future not like theirs
They had to fight to see that their parents are happy.

Proper home, dress well and eat well
That was in the 1960s
Rwandan girls were there for their family voluntarily
When things changed not for better but for worse.
They had to use their heads, hearts and their beauty
But fight for their family.
Had to do any work if it is physical or mental.
House girls and so on…
Marry without love.
But they had to fight for their families
Was struggle, at the end they got what they wanted.
What they fight for
Their struggle was not for nothing
Their families were at the top
And they were the winners.
Struggle of Rwandan girls.

TRANSITION

Transition can be to everyone
And transition can be everywhere
You born and be loved,
You are happy to be a child
When you are lucky to be in good care.
Especially the care of your parents
You grow up and are in transition
Transition of life and be aware of transition.
You had to work hard for your survival
And maybe you can be lucky in transition.
But sometimes you can be sad with life
You have to be in transition.
Since transition can be everywhere and to everyone.
You can love and be loved
And be happy to be in love
Within no time the love can disappear
That is transition.
Come, come, quickly, quickly.
Run, run
Pass here, oooh no pass there.
Transition is coming
It is changing
Indonesia

Pakistan

Oooh no, it is March/2011

Japan is changing,

Look outside

Houses are going

Cars are going

Bridges are breaking

Tsunami is here.

Flooding is here.

Earthquake

Transition can be to everyone and everywhere.

Transition is change.

TWIST OF LOVE

That is the day which is supposed to be the day on your memory. The day of lucky and happy accident.

When you met someone you loved, believed that you got what you wanted, what you dreamed for, maybe for long time waiting to come across it.

And then ready to fight for it for survive for ever, so that you can escape boredom and loneliness.

So that you can be with that beautiful feeling. To be with that love and feel that you are loved. When you feel that you breathe love and peace.

Twist of love.

You feel strong, bound and carefully threaded it and wove it into the fabric of new life. You celebrate that day and let yourself feel peace and power of love.

At a time when you look at each other's eyes in quiet position, time which didn't need any words.

Soft shy smiles and eyes talk themselves when only stories are between your hearts.

Hundred per cent see that you have a good new reason to allow yourself to live. Always see someone you love to be lovely and beautiful. And let love be where it is ready and where it is supposed to be.

Tell your friends, please don't touch it. That is when is high and fire of it, when is so strong than death. And see that is tree and you want your tree to be big and put down its roots, and happy to see your people sit under its shade.

That you are ready to guard it, so no one can shake it or chop it. Just be there and enjoy that good life with excitement.

Can't get enough of it.

Always hungry for it.

Always see it as flower blossoms.

Always see it as like a dove.

Hear beautifully and power of whisperings. And believe that you have a love of your heart of hearts and soul.

Twist of love.

See that you have a conclusion.

No more struggle.

No more sadness, since you are not alone by yourself.

You have someone who shields you from all the agonies.

And allow yourself to go completely in love without any frightening, see that you and your love are in safe protection.

That no harm could reach you.

<u>And then sometimes, with no time.</u>

No matter how long it took, short or long, one twist of love can turn out to be a monster. It will hurt you.

When it went in another direction, it will hurt you.

Especially if you trusted it.

And see that behind the screen was the smile of a shark!

Was bad betrayed and lies.

Absolutely felt sorry for yourself, at that time damaged by that relationship.

Effect is high in your heart and soul.

Disappointments when it is too high and scares your life.

Feel scared for good things and bad things.

And didn't want to believe that it is real.

You want to pretend that it is not.

Want something to help your brain.

Wish that it can be a bad dream

Don't know which style, which ladder you can use to be able to escape that bad feeling.

And see that there are no guarantees in life.

The cruel feelings.

Want to throw it away, far where you cannot and will not ever reach.

When you are unlucky to be in that twist of love.

Love of heart-breaking

Love of brutal hurt.

Love of loss trust.

Only tie up with mixed memories.

Love of artifice and arrogance.

Sometimes can be very hard to try again.

To be able to get courage enough to put your life together.

To try to love again and trust.

Unless if you are too strong and brave.

Good things of love, it gives people equality.

No matter how old, young or old.

How rich or poor.

It will praise you in the same level.

And both of you when it will turn its sword, it will hurt hard without any mercy.

Can be easier to never again.

When love is like a war
Easy to start
Hard to end.
Impossible to forget.
Twist of love.
2011.

WHO TO BLAME

Who to blame: authorities or parents?

About this problem with our young generation.
Internet, drugs, drink, knifes and pregnancy,
We have these stresses and suicide.

Who to blame; authority or parents?

I want to help my family by trying to see that my daughter
can start to have babies in early age so that we can have
a big benefit.

Ooo no no no. Not me, I have a very good idea to my
family; I will introduce pregnancy prevention to my
daughter at ten years old so that she can be able to have
enough time to have good education.

Now who is to blame: authority or parents?

Look, our youths from early age have to have sex education,
gay and lesbians so that they can know everything and
be easy to control themselves in young age.

Who to blame here: authority or parents?

Today is 2009, our country Britain has a big number of youth pregnancies, double that of Germany and three times that of France.

Don't panic, they are not going to be terrible; we have to have solution for our youth, for our society, and for our nation.

When we will be busy with internet, drugs, drink, knifes, stresses and suicide, our saviour will be near for us, we have very a good group who will get work to do, and help us by teaching us, treating us, making laws, serving the nation and saving us.

But I have no idea who to blame; if it is authority or parents.

Help me here.

HAPPY NEW YEAR

Members of Writers Without Borders
I wish you all the best in 2009 and beyond
To be the time of happiness for you and your family.
Including everyone who loves you.
I wish you to have a life without problems like President Mugabe in Zimbabwe has.
Without enemies like former America president W Bush has, in this year and afterwards to be lucky: like first black president of America Barack Obama.
To have long life and be respected like Nelson Mandela in S Africa.
To be brave like President Kagame in Rwanda.
To know that things without you can't have any valour, to work hard is not force or strength, it is heart.
To know that to be a good leader, a respected one, well known and famous, you don't have to be Hitler or G W Bush. And to be a good parent is not only to feed the child, but is also to guide the child.
Happy New Year Writers without Borders.

RWANDA WOMEN

Women of Rwanda your tears are felt
This act of genocide has destroyed your families
But has created a stronger more resilient race
Helpless you were to stop the rape of
Your daughters, sisters, mothers
And the slaughter of your men.
You have been slowly recovering since then
Through the aid of decent, caring men.
A stockpile of skeletal remains
Are living memory of your dead.
These infidels invaded your being.
Planted seeds of destruction, with evil intent
Yet you continue to humbly soldier on, rebuild lives
Preserving your dignity, maintaining respect.
This agonising shame cries out a thousand times.
Tears of anguish and of pain… of dying carers
Children orphaned yet again.
The world through the media is at your door
Their generosity's extending even more.
The family of man extend their arms
Embracing you, to soothe the pain.
Rest assured the world looks on and will be there once more
To share your trouble, to comfort you,

To show they care… yes, again and again you show that
You can put your families together
And your country to make it be the role model
Women of Rwanda we are with you and say
Never again will be never again.
That horrible will be no more.
That shame will be no more.

By Miss Kitty – 2013

WE ARE ONE

My people and I we are one
Bush travellers we are one.
Don't let human greed cruelty and stupidity hold you for
    ever.
Heal planet.
Let good people who have good heart heal planet
Let creator and spirit come back with my people.
Before river dying with chemical fertilisers
When the children were obey nature law from clans' elders
I saw half people their boats carried some humans
    imprisoned in chains
Horrible changes to me and my children.
Chained at the neck with other children who been taken
    away from our mama.
Matter of fact I didn't, I don't, even, didn't even know what
    she look like.
When half people tell us that we will banish you from this
    land. Die here or walk north.
If you will walk you will walk no further. Up to the camp,
    up to the prison. We have no more words for you.
Sometimes the flames and smoke prevented the confused
    half-people from seeing the Kangaroo people until too
    late.

Warrior survival… No more natural process of celebration.

The crucial understanding was reinforced through dancing and ritual to make the young full and strong for country clan and sacred law.

To wipe my people.

They used what they called civilisation and progress.

Their new knowledge necessitated the development of the tool of writing, and the science of mathematics. They wanted uninhabited by humans without the so can salter interference of full people demanding respect.

How they suffered starvation, illness and debilitating discrimination measures designed to ensure that they could not escape the system administered by the department of native affairs to be able to kill them in slow motion but in clue and evil way also were that of separating families etc… all of that in their own country.

Word comes through him, not from him.

System for recording and registering something called writing many details of the new lifestyle.

Bulling becomes a feature of their behaviour.

Heavy work in the camps. Such things were aliens to traditional lifestyle.

Full people – half people.

Control everybody and kill dissenters.

Death was reasonable fate to those who failed to carry out the wishes of those called chief, shaman or bull man.

Unacceptable to full people clan and sacred law.

Black people have to beg and lose pride, create hard hatred and dislike each other.

Brutal salve societies evolving from the practice of

agriculture. When greed and profit are acceptable, the trees disappear. And where the earth is poisoned, and air and water become dirty.

Competition and wars.

For creation or observance of any kinship restrictions on procreation. Creation itself become target of resentment, and were their enemy according to the serpent's law, none of them were entitled to life.

Many of their senior chiefs and thousands of half-people had perished in difficult and shameful circumstances because of the serpent's restrictive laws. When so-called full people favoured by the so-called sacred serpent.

Human experience is stronger than any other education.

Through our elders natural laws which form our universe and have only to do with creation. Those not taken by small pox and other imported diseases were subjected to massacres. And many were given poisoned flour as food.

My people even today they teach their children to share even before the young learn to walk.

Songs and stories of the proud survivor warriors of the lands.

The practice of invasion and theft of country was totally outside my people's experience of respectful human behaviour.

Unbroken line of blood through our parents since people became human, right to hunt and share with neighbours.

My responsibilities extend through spiritual connections clan and inter-clan relationships.

Clan, country and neighbours traditional lifestyle to maximise the health of the land, its species and clan group. Invader, who has no spiritual connection to the land, has no secret of bush fires.

Invader, who has no spiritual connection to the land, has no secret of bush fires.

"But the continent of writing did not have to reflect absolute truth. And their influence would become folk lore and last through time, long after the author were dead."

My Kungulu people. The elders would usually be consulted when matters of importance arose. That was their obligation.

Each group knew they had no right to take resource from any other clan country or disrespect clan boundaries.

This is good place.

This is Kungulu ground.

When they are done with grieving we are here. We are ready to become full people again to sing to gather with our soil, the trees and waters welcome our children back to country and sing up protection.

Dark brothers, first Australian race.

Soon you will take your rightful place

In the brotherhood long waited for,

Fringe-dweller no more.

Sore, sore, the tears you shed no more. When hope seemed folly and justice dead.

Was the long night weary?

Look up, dark band, the down is at hand.

Me and my people we are one.

From: The River Story. To empower the powerless. In the respect of late Ross Watson

WHAT A SHOCK?

Now on August 2014 I put my pen down.
To talk about this shock
We are in bad shock which is too horrible.
Yes it is not the first time and is not second either
But this time it got us, it got a name.
No more to ask about it, it pushed itself to be known
International
The whole world now is scared about it.
And now, the truth, they are standing by
In case that evil comes to their doors
This killer is not sickness like others we knew before
Not even like Aids
This Ebola is killing in its style and it has its own laws!
You African people, I am here to tell you to change some of
    your cultures.
No more hand shakings
I refuse you to take care of your loved ones
Especially when you saw that I get her or him
I am evil who doesn't have mercy on anyone
Even doctors fear me, because I don't give a damn
If you can joke with me I can wipe out your villages like a
    tsunami
I will make you even fear to bury the dead

My victims.

That is how much I am too dangerous

That is how much I put fear into your brain

Especially when you saw that I got her or him

You have to know that this horrible killer is in part of Africa.

In that continent which is one of third world

Meaning one of poor continents

When it is known to hold a lot of richness.

But still with poor economy, poor facilities and poor technologies

This killer can be too easy to be worse.

They started to say that Africa is the original of this evil.

And yes that is where we see it any way.

They say that exactly the same like Aids!

When they tried to pin it to Africa continent to be its original

The proof of Ebola: because the people of that part of Africa

They eat monkeys. No, no. They don't believe to be the reason.

When was it their favourite food for centuries?

Wait a minute. Can it be manmade? To try and see how African people can be wiped out and get Africa for free! Watch out friend. Don't tell me history.

No one knows, at least not now.

If they are something to be out, on the light, might take years.

Ebola is too evil which is refusing its victims to say bye to loved ones.

What a shock!

What death

What evil

Ebola is too horrible.

ACKNOWLEDGMENTS

I would like to express my heart felt gratitude to several people who brought about the completion of this book. Their ideas, encouragement and wise pieces of advice contributed a lot in making this book.

My thoughts and hard work have matured into this piece of my poems, which is the fruit of my patriotism.

Without the love of the gifted people who are around me, family and friends, I would not have had the courage to produce this book. I first of all thank my co-members of Writers Without Borders who have shown me the way, and helped me to have my confidence to be able to become a proper writer.

I extend my deepest gratitude to my niece Domitira Mukarutesi Ngamije for her encouragements, happy to help whoever she can. Thanks to her and Bosco Ngabonzima for translating some of my poems.

Many thanks to Sue Brown, Inga Durrani and the late Saeeda Younus for correction and encouragements. Many thanks to Predencia who is always happy to show me the way. And always I thank my children and my friends who are there for me for whatever I do, and proud of me when I reach one more step, something which pushes me to go and go ahead.

I thank my parents Bagorebeza and Sinzi my great parents for their angels who sat with me into the early hours of the morning, telling me that I can.

Many thanks to my God who is guiding me, and always gives me hope and patience to go ahead and do more.

I would like to express my heart-felt thanks to acknowledge my neighbour George Conner, this Jamaica gentleman who is always happy to help where he can, voluntary. I see him as a good brother to me, if it was not for his help, it would not be easy for me to put this book out.

Thank you George, my God bless you always.